# Recovering Politics, Civilization, and the Soul

**Other Books of Interest from St. Augustine's Press**

Daniel J. Mahoney, *The Other Solzhenitsyn:*
*Telling the Truth about a Misunderstood Writer and Thinker*

Pierre Manent, *Beyond Radical Secularism:*
*How France and the Christian West Should Respond to the Islamic Challenge*

Pierre Manent, *Seeing Things Politically:*
*Interviews with Benedicte Delorme-Montini*

Roger Scruton, *The Aesthetic Understanding:*
*Essays in the Philosophy of Art and Culture*

Roger Scruton, *Art and Imagination: A Study in the Philosophy of Mind*

Roger Scruton, *The Meaning of Conservatism*

Roger Scruton, *On Hunting*

Roger Scruton, *Perictione in Colophon*

Roger Scruton, *Philosopher on Dover Beach: Essays*

Roger Scruton, *The Politics of Culture and Other Essays*

Roger Scruton, *Xanthippic Dialogues*

Rémi Brague, *The Anchors in the Heavens*

Rémi Brague, *Moderately Modern*

Marvin R. O'Connell, *Telling Stories that Matter: Memoirs and Essays*

Josef Pieper, *Traditional Truth, Poetry, Sacrament:*
*For My Mother, on her 70th Birthday*

Alexandre Kojève, *The Concept, Time, and Discourse*

David Lowenthal, *Slave State: Rereading Orwell's 1984*

Nalin Ranasinghe, *The Confessions of Odysseus*

Will Morrisey, *Shakespeare's Politic Comedy*

John Poch, *God's Poems: The Beauty of Poetry and the Christian Imagination*

Gabriel Marcel, *The Invisible Threshold: Two Plays by Gabriel Marcel*

Stanley Rosen, *The Language of Love: An Interpretation of Plato's Phaedrus*

Winston Churchill, *The River War*

# Recovering Politics, Civilization, and the Soul

## ESSAYS ON PIERRE MANENT AND ROGER SCRUTON
### DANIEL J. MAHONEY

ST. AUGUSTINE'S PRESS

South Bend, Indiana

Manufactured in the United States of America.

1  2  3  4  5  6   27  26  25  24  23  22

**Library of Congress Control Number: 2022945614**

Paperback ISBN: 978-1-58731-708-8
Ebook ISBN: 978-1-58731-709-5

∞ The paper used in this publication meets the minimum requirements of the American National Standard for Information Sciences – Permanence of Paper for Printed Materials, ANSI Z39.48-1984.

St. Augustine's Press
www.staugustine.net

# Table of Contents

## Introduction

# RECOVERING POLITICS, CIVILIZATION, AND THE SOUL

There is no more fundamental task that lies before us than a self-conscious effort to recover the meaning of politics, civilization, and the soul for this (or any other) time. Not politics as a diabolical realm of power-seeking and "domination" rooted in will-to-power, but the "ruling and being ruled in turn," as Aristotle called it, made possible by the uniquely human capacity to speak and reason about "the advantageous and the just." If politics is unthinkable without conflict, it is defined above all by the enduring and humanizing imperative to "put reason and actions in common." Politics so understood is at once light years from the violent mastery that defines despotism, the metaphysically mad dream of a "solution" to the human condition at the heart of all revolutionary and utopian temptations, and the anarchist and libertarian reverie that freely associating individuals can escape the arduous requirements of moral and civic virtue, debate, and disputation. Politics rightly understood is not reducible to morality. It is at the same time incompatible with frenzied moralism and all ideological projects to move beyond truth and falsehood, good and evil. If politics isn't identical with ethics, it is an essentially moral enterprise.

By civilization I have in mind that state of human flourishing where ordered liberty is tied to law and self-limitation, and where progress in the arts and sciences, and in economic productivity more broadly, is accompanied by a sober appreciation of human imperfection and the fragility of all human achievements. Civilized human beings must combine a certain confidence in the ability of human beings to govern themselves, and to achieve great things, with a pronounced appreciation of the sempiternal drama of good and evil in every heart and soul, and even of the fragility of civilization itself. In authentic civilized existence, reformation must be tied to conservation, in Burke's famous words. Civilized human beings should never succumb to the allure of some revolutionary or ideological "Year Zero" where all will be made anew. That is the path of political and spiritual perdition, of murderous negation. The Kingdom of Heaven, in decisive respects, is not of this world.

There can also be no recovery of free politics and of our civilized patrimony without a renewed appreciation of the human soul as the locus of free will, personhood, moral agency, personal responsibility, and human dignity as such. The soul is not a metaphor or a poetic fiction. It is the "I" in the I-Thou relationship of which Martin Buber famously spoke, it is the self (but more than a self) that exercises the virtues, moral and intellectual, and that experiences remorse when we human beings act or choose poorly or even inexcusably. It is the seat of our consciousness and it is what a face and speech give expression to when we encounter other human beings in familial, social, and political settings. It is inseparable from the *logos*—the human capacity for speech and reason—that makes political life possible for the political animals that human beings are. Without it, philosophical reflection is impossible. It is tied to character and character formation, and it is what endures as we physically age and endlessly metabolize. Contrary to a widespread fiction of our time, it is we who think, speak, and act, not our brains as essential as they are to our embodied personhood.

We "thinking reeds," as Pascal called us, have no identity, dignity, or capacity for thought or action without the human soul. To deny it is to deny our access to self-knowledge and a common world. "Nothing-but-tery," the reductive explaining away of the soul as nothing but matter in motion, free will and consciousness as nothing but illusions of "folk psychology," and God as a superstitious projection of infantile fantasies, gravely distorts reality. It is also a recipe for personal and civilizational self-destruction. As Alexis de Tocqueville and Walker Percy both asked with consternation, why do modern intellectuals, scientists, and philosophers take such pride and pleasure in explaining away their own powers of ratiocination? Creatively exercising the remarkable powers of the "angel" in man, they are delighted to proclaim themselves nothing but "brutes." That, too, is the path of spiritual perdition. It is anything but realistic and "scientific," whatever its scientistic dogmatists say.

The book you have before you hopes to pursue another more truthful and humanizing path. It takes its bearing from the late English philosopher

2

and man of letters Roger Scruton (1944–2020) and the contemporary French political philosopher Pierre Manent (who was born in 1949). In my judgment, they are the contemporary philosophers and political thinkers who demonstrate how we can recover the continuity of civilization, the dignity of the political vocation, and an appreciation of the ensouled human person. They are philosophers who resist the late modern dogma, and it is a dogma, that the Good is absolutely *unsupported* in the nature of things. By opening themselves to what Scruton, following Husserl, called the "life-world," the world of lived experience, and what Manent calls the imperatives of action ("What are we to do?"), as opposed to abstract theorizing, they have recovered a sound grounding for politics, civilization, and the soul in the world right before us and within us.

To be sure, there are differences of some importance between these two men and thinkers. Scruton is more concerned with saving the residues of high culture and our inherited tradition; Manent with renewing the possibilities of human action and practical reason. Scruton owes much to Kant and Burke; Manent to Aristotle, St. Thomas, Tocqueville, and (with important qualifications) Leo Strauss. One is unmistakably English; the other strikingly French. As partisans of the self-governing nation, and of the plural civilization that is the West, that is exactly as it should be. In this case, an American will do the mediation.

This book is attentive to their affinities perhaps even more than their differences. Both deny, in Pierre Manent's words from a 2019 address, that "humanity" in and of itself has any "concrete political reality." They both see in the national form not only the indispensable instrument for democratic self-government but the only viable instrument for keeping justice and force together, to cite a famous and memorable formulation from Pascal's *Pensées*. Both have thought seriously, even profoundly, about how to conjugate the secular state with the broader Christian inheritance of the Western world. For Scruton, the neighbor-love so beautifully evoked by Christ in the Gospels "makes sense" on the political plane "only if there is also a neighborhood in which it can be freely and safely exercised," as he put it in a 2017 article in *Law and Liberty*. For Manent, the self-governing nation owes much to the European Christian search for a political form that avoided the "immensity" of empire and the "puniness" of the city-state. That is the political *via media* that Christianity made possible.

Both Manent and Scruton see "care of the soul" as the great imperative, at once moral and intellectual, uniting classical and Christian wisdom and separating it from every ideological project to free human beings
from the challenge to put in order our souls. To do so, is to live in light
of the cardinal virtues—courage, moderation, justice, and prudence—
virtues that give strength and definition to a life well-lived. By allowing
the phenomena to come to sight unimpeded by scientific reductionism,
ideological utopianism, and a humanitarianism at odds with both civic
loyalties and transcendental religion, they help restore the ties that connect ordinary experience with discerning philosophical reflection. They
both admirably fulfill what Leo Strauss called the highest practical task
of political philosophy: to defend sound practice against bad theory. Neither identifies philosophy with moral transgression or with an antinomianism that forgets that sound practice is in effect a "second nature" for
human beings. The reckless disregard of traditional wisdom is far from
philosophical. It shows contempt for the accumulated wisdom of humankind. It has nothing to do with the search for truth. Negation is completely devoid of intellectual *eros* and thus is deeply at odds with
philosophy rightly understood.

Manent and Scruton are also profoundly countercultural, and not a
little courageous, in their openness to the wisdom inherent in the Christian
religion. Both are philosophers who treat religion with some circumspection
and with a great deal of respect. In his latest book, *Pascal et la proposition
chrétienne*, to be published by Editions Grasset in the fall of 2022, Manent
emphasizes the radical impoverishment of collective life and the human
soul that occurs when spiritually complacent men and women forget "the
most high and urgent question that the rational animal" that is man is capable of posing, the question of God, inseparable from "the Question" of
"the meaning and urgency of life." Late modern man confuses the Christian
proposition that forgets neither Adam's sin nor Christ's sacrifice on the
Cross, with a complacent belief in human resemblance and self-sufficiency,
and in egalitarian politics separated from any need for Divine Grace to save
man from his incorrigible sinfulness. Compassion and sentimentality replace charity. A naïve and facile faith in human unity or brotherhood
substitutes for faith in God and demanding care for the soul. Cheap grace,
indeed, and bad politics to boot.

Scruton's engagement with Christianity is perhaps more qualified than Manent's. Scruton oscillates between a defense of the "sacred" rooted in the life-world with an openness to the transcendence glimpsed "at the edge of things." But in the face of man, which strikingly reveals the reality of personhood and the soul, Scruton sees intimations of God himself, "the face of God" who informs "the soul of the world." Scruton could not imagine a truly reasonable account of the human world that reduced "the holy, the forbidden, the sacred, the profane, and the sentimental" to something other than themselves. In the Anglican liturgy and the commemoration of the Lord's Supper, Scruton saw sacramental access to a holy realm where the true meaning of sacrifice, repentance, forgiveness, and communion with God are more fully revealed. In them, Scruton saw "a purifying rite" and "a visitation of the transcendental," as he put in a luminous 2016 lecture ("The Sacred, the Profane, and the Desecrated") at Westminster Abbey posthumously published in the Summer 2021 issue of *The European Conservative*.

In the study that follows, all this will be explored and more. Against the dominant spirit of repudiation, we will rediscover the path of affirmation. Against ideology and moralistic fanaticism, which is the frenzied side of moral relativism, we will see humane political reason at work. Against atheism, whether fervent or indifferent, we will see what is entailed in genuine openness to the Good—and God. And in contrast to the regnant religion of humanity, with its facile cosmopolitanism and failure to engage the breadth and depths of the soul, we will see how moral and political philosophy can allow us to recover all the resources of the soul.

This is no mere scholarly study. These two men and thinkers have been very important to me in my own search for a true understanding of politics, civilization, and the soul. I am blessed to count them among my friends. And in their respective modes of opening themselves to the truth about the soul and the world, I see a gift for all who still care about receptivity to truth and the cultivation of our civilized inheritance and common home.

This book has been many years in the making. The book forms a self-conscious whole but each essay can be fruitfully read on its own terms. Engaging over many decades with the writings and philosophical reflection of these two esteemed thinkers has greatly informed and deepened my own reflection. And having Pierre Manent and Roger Scruton as friends and

5

interlocutors has been the gift of a lifetime. Thanks, too, to Mark Dooley, Dan Cullen, and Fisher Derderien for freely sharing their thoughts and insights about Sir Roger's contributions to philosophy, political thought, and humane letters. Giulio de Ligio, Ralph Hancock, and Paul Seaton, old and trusted friends, have been precious interlocutors about every theme related to this book and almost every matter. They fully share my admiration for, and indebtedness to, the intellectual contributions of Pierre Manent and Sir Roger Scruton. My friend and colleague Geoffrey Vaughan is a line-editor par excellence and a source of invariably good advice, editorial and otherwise. Thanks, too, to Jack Fowler and Marc Guerra, whose friendship and encouragement are always steadfast and invaluable. I am also deeply grateful to Gabrielle Maher whose help typing and collating quotations and in formatting this volume is an absolutely essential part of the "process." And many thanks to the editors of *The New Criterion, Perspectives on Political Science, The Hungarian Review, Law and Liberty*, the *Political Science Reviewer*, and *The European Conservative* for publishing earlier versions of some of these chapters. Last but not least, thanks to Katie Godfrey and Benjamin Fingerhut at St. Augustine's Press for their ongoing support and encouragement. St. Augustine's is a blessed isle of serious thought, reflection, and artful publishing in a growing sea of intellectual debasement. May they long prosper.

Daniel J. Mahoney
Clinton, Massachusetts
July 7, 2022

# Chapter 1
# ROGER SCRUTON:
# DEFENDER OF THE SOUL AND CIVILIZATION

The death of Roger Scruton on January 12, 2020, came as a surprise to me. I knew he was fighting a terrible battle with cancer, but I was under the misimpression that he had turned a corner for the better. We had been intermittently in touch by email in recent months, and I admired his spirit and his continuing vigor and alertness. He had been honored throughout the fall of 2019 by the Czech, Polish, and Hungarian governments, respectively, in a welcome display of gratitude for his courageous efforts to aid the intellectual underground in each of those countries in the decade before the revolutions of 1989 that felled European communism, seemingly once and for all. That story is best told in Chapter Five of *Conversations with Roger Scruton* (2016), discourses ably initiated and conducted by the Irish philosopher Mark Dooley. I know that these honors meant a great deal to Roger, as one can immediately tell by looking at the photographs of him as he was about to address the Czech Senate in the fall. This English patriot, this able theoretician of the dignity of territorial democracy and national self-government, was also at home in the great and ancient nations of Eastern Europe, in his beloved France (a second intellectual home that took great interest in his work in the last few years), in the United States (where he had so many friends and admirers), and even in Lebanon (whose decimation at the hands of assorted fanatics he chronicled in one of his first and best books, *A Land Held Hostage: Lebanon and the West*). As he argued in his splendid address upon receiving the Western Civilization Award from the Intercollegiate Studies Institute in the fall of 2019 (given his illness, his remarks were delivered by Skype), to be a friend and partisan of Western civilization is to be a friend and partisan of civilization, simply. His *oikophilia*, his principled love of home, was in truth a proposition for all mankind. It was never narrowly particularistic, chauvinistic, or blind to the accomplishments of other peoples and civilizations.

I followed Roger's work intermittently in the years after 1980. He won me over almost immediately with his elegant and persuasive defense of the human soul against every form of reductionism and his eloquent and passionate opposition to what he so aptly called the "culture of repudiation." I must have quoted that phrase in fifteen of my articles and books, never tiring of a line that captured the phenomenon of Western self-hatred and self-recrimination so perfectly. He gave a fitting name to a debilitating spirit we confront every day.

We first met at a three-day conference sponsored by ISI in Oxford in the early 2000s, where Scruton brilliantly articulated the relationships among Edmund Burke's aesthetics, conservatism, and defense of ordered liberty. Sometime after that I read Scruton's autobiographical *Gentle Regrets* (2005), which left a deep impression on me. As a student and admirer of Burke, Tocqueville, Raymond Aron, and Charles de Gaulle, I was captivated by Roger's account of his turn to conservatism beginning, in May 1968, with his front-row seat to a Paris on fire with nihilistic rage and reckless admiration for Castroite and Maoist despotism. Scruton, reading de Gaulle's captivating *Mémoires de Guerre*, saw in contrast what it meant to love and preserve a great people and nation. His experience of revolutionary antinomianism in Paris, his turn to Burke's aesthetics and politics, and his deep and principled anti-totalitarianism were all of a piece. And how rare it was to meet an Englishman who was a *bona fide* Gaullist or Gaullist fellow-traveler. I once commented to him that he cited de Gaulle far more than he mentioned or praised another candidate for conservative hero, Winston Churchill.

One other thing in *Gentle Regrets* particularly caught my attention. Scruton, it seems, was evolving from a humane and dignified, but still largely secular, personalism (largely influenced by Kant) to a more open and sympathetic stance toward the Christian religion. To this day, many see in him "a cultural Anglican" whose love of beauty and high culture went hand in hand with a rather sophisticated atheism. This judgment cannot be more false, as I will attempt to explain in various places in this book.

I met Roger again in the spring of 2015 at a conference at Rhodes College in Memphis, Tennessee, sponsored by his good friend, exegete, and admirer—and my friend, too—the political theorist Dan Cullen. By that time, I had reviewed half a dozen of Roger's works, seeing in them a well-spring of impressive conservative and philosophical wisdom. Given my work on Solzhenitsyn (and to a lesser extent Václav Havel), I immediately took to his profound and lyrical novel *Notes from Underground*, published by Beaufort Books in 2014 (and analyzed at length later in this book). Here was a book that got to the heart of totalitarian mendacity while depicting the efforts of a small minority of self-respecting Czechs to "live not by lies," in Solzhenitsyn's inestimable phrase. At the conference, I presented on the book, one that continues to preoccupy me. Better than any recent book I knew, I argued, Scruton's novel illustrated the profound truth that human beings are above all persons to be respected and not playthings to be endlessly manipulated by ideologists, technocrats, and soulless bureaucrats. His unforgettable characters—Jan Reichl, Betka Palková, Father Pavel—were less sainted "dissidents" than imperfect human beings who attempted to maintain their personal integrity and moral dignity in a phantasmagorical world marked by the loss of personal responsibility and moral agency. Scruton wrote with passionate sympathy for these men and women who refused to succumb to the ideological Lie even as he avoided anything resembling hagiography. The Czech philosopher Jan Patočka's "solidarity of the shattered" became palpable in Scruton's artful and moving book. Scruton was pleased by my engagement with his book and encouraged me to develop it into a full-blown essay. I did so in the summer of 2019, writing a twenty-six-page engagement with *Notes from Underground* that appeared in *VoegelinView* in the fall of 2019, and that appears in revised form later in this book. I was touched and pleased when Roger recommended my essay to his readers and admirers in his fall newsletter from "Scrutopia," his farm and intellectual enclave in Wiltshire, England, which brings together, as Dooley has so deftly put it, "farmers and philosophers, Wagner and wine, Aristotle and animals." It doesn't get better than this—a conservative utopia that could be someplace precisely because it respects persons as such. Scrutopia was the very embodiment of *oikophilia* and a living reproach to the self-contempt Scruton labelled *oikophobia*.

Cullen and I also plotted to bring Roger and the contemporary French political philosopher Pierre Manent together. We almost succeeded when I was president of the New England Political Science Association in 2016, but poor Roger was too injured to travel after he fell off a horse on his Sunday Hill Farm. Scruton and Manent were, in my view, the most thoughtful and persuasive defenders of humane national loyalty and national self-government writing at the time. They thought deeply about human nature, practical reason, and the natural moral law, themes superseded by the regnant relativism and nihilism. They both had contempt for the post-political nihilism and antinomianism arising out of the May events in Paris in 1968. Both defended the secular state while doing full justice to the "Christian mark" of Europe, to cite Manent's suggestive phrase. The exploration of these themes is at the center of this book.

They finally came together for a dialogue at a conference sponsored by the Institut Thomas More in Paris at the end of May 2019. I, alas, had to miss the event I was so looking forward to because my nephew was getting married in Vermont at the same time. But my friend Giulio de Ligio reports that it was a most memorable conversation, with both agreeing on the absolute indispensability of the self-governing nation-state and the need for a properly "conservative" attitude to recover "what we love and the capacity for action." The first is Scruton's preeminent theme, the second Manent's. One citing Burke, the other Tocqueville and Aristotle, these two philosophers (they surely deserve the name) give one hope that the cause of Western liberty can be sustained and revitalized if we draw on the humanizing wisdom of the past to recover the prospects for reasonable thought and action in the future. A recovery and revitalization of old wisdom is a precondition for the reassertion of reasonable choice—and thoughtful action—in an era marked by debilitating relativism and angry moralism. Together, Scruton and Manent point in a much more humane, truthful, and salutary direction. As we shall see, these affinities and divergences are at once complementary and instructive.

As others have pointed out, Scruton's conservatism has both a metaphysical and empirical dimension. Long before he returned to a rather distinctive Christian affirmation, he rejected every form of materialistic and scientistic reductionism. At the center of his thought was the *life world*, the world of concrete experience where humans came to sight as *persons*. This was a world marked by freedom and accountability, and not a web of necessity that knows nothing of the self-conscious, dignified, acting person. But for Scruton, human beings were embodied or "incarnate" persons, and not *noumenal* selves, to use Kant's term, free from all natural and external limitations. The free and accountable human being accepts legitimate authority and the limits inherent in the human condition with grace and equanimity. He does not confuse them, as Michel Foucault and the postmodern Left so recklessly do, with coercion and imperious domination. Where the Left sees only "false consciousness," Scruton affirmed legitimate authority—moral, intellectual, and political—that is the other side of human freedom. His writings on sexual desire (including his 1986 book of that name) are profoundly personalistic, even if not expressly Christian. Still, a self-declared "godless conservative" before his return to religion so luminously described in *Gentle Regrets*, he nonetheless saw that sexual virtue "reconstitutes the physical urge as an interpersonal feeling." Incarnate persons do not stand in an instrumental relation to their bodies: as embodied persons, fidelity to the self-restraint inherent in sexual morality allows genuine communion with another human being. A truly human "sexual ethic" recognizes the reality of "moral pollution" and the obliteration of personhood inherent in large-scale pornography.

I have already referred to Scruton's courageous opposition to the monstrosity which was communist totalitarianism, even in its somewhat less malignant form in East-Central Europe in the years after the death of Stalin. This noble witness for truth and liberty had little or nothing to do with an abstract attachment to "human rights" or political democracy. A world reduced to rights is almost as tyrannical as a world dominated by arbitrary command (a countercultural view also shared by Pierre Manent). Rather, Scruton saw in ideological mendacity, in the regime of the Lie, a self-conscious effort to deface the very personhood of human beings. As in earlier waves of Jacobin and Communist terror, he saw exactly what the "revolutionary mentality" took aim at, namely the dignity of "the animal in whom the light of reason shines, and who looks at us from eyes which tell of freedom." For decent and humane politics, and true philosophy and religion, that direct experience of the human face, of eyes that ask for human respect and affection, illumines the reality of the sacred, as well as the necessity of both moral accountability and political reciprocity, of the "ruling and being ruled in turn" first heralded by Aristotle. But modern ideological revolution "leads to murder for the simple reason that it rids the world of the experience"—of the self or soul, the incarnate person—"upon which the refusal to murder depends," to quote Scruton's remarkable 1989 essay "Man's Second Obedience: Reflections on the French Revolution," which appeared in *Philosopher on Dover Beach: Essays*. We shall return to that essay, brimming with insights, in the course of our discussions.

As a visiting student in France in 1968, Scruton understood Charles de Gaulle—the "old fascist" denounced by the *soixante-huitards*—as the noble guardian of the French inheritance, and he saw the radical students as middle-class brats, inebriated by ideology, who knew only how to tear down and destroy. Edmund Burke gave theoretical expression to Scruton's natural piety: revolutionaries displayed "self-righteous contempt" for the wisdom of the ancestors, and they gave little thought to their responsibilities toward the yet to be born despite all their talk about "progress" and the "future." They transgressed against the great primordial contract, so eloquently affirmed by Burke in his *Reflections on the Revolution in France*, that reflects the great and enduring "partnership between the dead, the living, and the unborn." That primordial contract, and not a misplaced confidence in inevitable moral progress, is the precondition for a renewal of the Platonic commitment to "care of the soul . . . which would also be a care for absent generations." In Scruton's mix of concerns, affirmations, and judgments, Kant's emphasis on the free and morally accountable person, Burke's politics of prudence and of civilizational continuity, Plato's defense of "care of the soul," and an Aristotelian defense of moderation and practical reason go hand in hand, with Kant predominating in philosophy and Burke in politics. In Scruton's thought and writing, multiple and overlapping philosophical, moral, and political traditions come alive—not to proffer a misplaced call to liberation but to provide tender care and intellectual support for those aspects of our inheritance that are in the process of being lost: self-government, a disinterested appreciation of beauty, a commitment to home against the railings of *oikophobes*, and a conception of the person that does not explain away the ennobling experiences at the foundation of our humanity.

In a nutshell, Scruton shows that high philosophy has a duty to come to the defense of the home and starting point of all incarnate persons. I have my doubts about Scruton's "cognitive dualism," his Kant-inspired view that the incarnate person and the web of causal necessity exist in two spheres that are in important points distinct. This seems strained to me, a rare concession on Scruton's part to the priority of abstract theory (a scientific account) over lived experience. But Scruton never sacrificed the realm of personal knowledge, or the inner life of the soul, to a reductionism that abolished personhood as such. He was a learned and eloquent critic of materialism and scientific reductionism in all their forms.

And see how Scruton brings to light, against faux sophisticates, the fact that architecture should aim both to be fitting and to endure. He eloquently exposes the "self-centered" character of modernist public building: Boston City Hall (an ugly monstrosity that I know well), London's South Bank, and New York's Lincoln Center are indeed all "crumbling dysfunctional survivals from the age of ill-considered and temporary things." But Scruton is never simply or primarily negative when he addresses matters of common culture. He always puts forward a positive vision of the fitting, the useful, the beautiful, and the things that are made to endure.

Following but modifying the Kant of the *Third Critique*, Scruton defends the "disinterested pleasure" that true art gives to a rational and sentient being. It is precisely because we are beings with "language, self-consciousness, practical reason, and moral judgment" that we can look out and appreciate the beauty in the world in an "alert and disinterested" (but not uninterested) way. And, as Scruton writes in his 2009 book *Beauty* (written to accompany his documentary on the same subject), aesthetic experience and judgment are never truly relative or arbitrary. The "experience of beauty," Scruton tells us, is "well founded." Against the scoffers who deny the presence of beauty in the soul, Scruton reaffirms the classical insight that for a free being, the incarnate person to whom we have freely made mention, "there is right feeling, right experience and right judgment just as much as right action."

Kant's *Critique of Judgment* leads Scruton back to a more classical view of the capacity of the human soul to connect with the natural order of things. Scruton is never doctrinaire or dogmatic when he recovers the intimations of transcendence that we experience in our souls and that peer at us from "the edge of things." Unlike Kant, however, for Scruton there is no absolute and impassable divide between the noumenal and the phenomenal, the metaphysical and the empirical. Human beings are neither matter in motion, brains that are compelled to act independent of human agency, nor noumenal selves who need not respect the requirements of the world around them. And in contradistinction to the regnant "neuro-babble," as he provocatively called it, he fully appreciated that persons think, reflect, and decide, and not their brains. His "cognitive dualism," whatever its other deficiencies, left room for all that.

Perhaps it is in his writings on music, ample as they are, that Scruton best shows us how beauty of the first order allows us to obtain a glimpse within our souls and the world, of that sublime encounter where "the intersection of the timeless and time" becomes available to human beings. Once we recognize ourselves as persons and remain faithful to all the intimations available to the soul, scientism and aesthetic relativism reveal themselves to be desperate efforts to escape from the freedom, accountability, and judgment that marks persons as persons. Scientism, carried to its logical conclusions, aims to eviscerate both self-consciousness and self-knowledge, and "care of the soul" in any meaningful sense of the term. Those who affirm it use the ample powers of the soul to eviscerate its presence in the human world.

I have no doubt that Roger Scruton lived and died as a Christian. He had his doubts and knew that philosophy could only provide so much support for an explicitly Christian affirmation. But he knew that "our consciousness of consciousness" made us aware of "a light shining in the center" of our very being as humans. His fundamental stance was that of the life world and not that of the causal necessity that explained away human consciousness as if it were a barrier to true scientific understanding. Who, after all, is this "I" doing the knowing? About that, reductionists have nothing compelling to say. The freedom, responsibility, and mutual accountability of human beings with souls meant that Martin Buber's "I–Thou" relationship was the one proper to human beings, who are never mere objects. And the light of reason and accountability at the heart of the incarnate person perhaps pointed to "the 'I' of God, in which we all stand judged, and from which love and freedom flow." Without too much fear and trembling, Scruton returned to the Anglican Church, playing the organ in his little rural parish in Wiltshire. As Father Pavel argues in the most moving terms in *Notes from Underground*, God may be "silent," or largely silent, but he is not dead. He is present in suffering, in the light of the soul that still shines from human eyes, and in "the solidarity" of those who affirm goodness and truth against the all-pervasive lies of a totalitarian political order. Even in ordinary things, in the "everydayness" that Martin Heidegger looked at with suspicion, one can glean the irreducible dignity of the human person which points to both moral accountability and judgment—and to a transcendent source of this realm where freedom and responsibility rule, not some inhuman necessity beyond good and evil.

But Scruton was never a sentimentalist, a political utopian, or a believer in the prospects for making the "kingdom of Ends"—subjects without form or limits—the basis of a community of incarnate persons. Just as he resisted Communist totalitarianism and every call to appease the West's implacable foes during the Cold War, he too believed that free peoples were obliged to defend citizenship in a territorial democracy against demands for *sharia* and religious conformity. And he strikingly preferred "cheerful drinking," as he called it, to "censorious abstinence" (Scruton and the great Churchill had that in common). He believed, as he put it in a late essay called "Defending the West," that we, the citizens of Western liberal societies, "must respond" to the violence of Islamist terrorists "with whatever force is required to contain it, if we can." Scruton defended a secular state whose home was territorial democracy informed by humane national loyalty and the broader Judeo-Christian inheritance of the West. But in the private sphere, he counseled a "spirit of forgiveness" that freed the soul from the endless cycle of anger and recrimination (René Girard was an influence here). But he knew this was "the hard part of the task—hard to perform, hard to endorse and hard to recommend to others." He never advocated pacifism, since the weak and defenseless must always be defended against the unscrupulous enemies of freedom and civilization. Out of self-respect we must defend our home and the decent and free political arrangements to be found there.

In Scruton's view of the world, rights are always accompanied by obligations, and love of home (and civilization more broadly) is rooted in respect and affection for actual persons. In Scruton's myriad writings, fifty books and countless articles and columns, the metaphysical grounds of human dignity come together with a politics of prudence, a melding one might say of Kant's personalism with Aristotle's and Burke's appeals to practical reason. In all his books and writings, the sacred, the person, and the freedom and accountability of human beings are defended against the totalitarian temptation and every form of scientistic reductionism. These were Scruton's great "transcendentals" that gave us a glimpse of "eternity" in time.

I concluded my review of *Conversations with Roger Scruton* ("Dialogues in Scrutopia," *The New Criterion*, May 2017) on a hopeful note. At the end of that charming and instructive book, Dooley and Scruton expressed (qualified) hope that the days when Roger was considered an "intellectual pariah" were long behind him. Many well-deserved honors had come, including knighthood. He was now a member of the esteemed British Academy and the Royal Society of Literature (the latter meant much more to him given how much he valued excellent writing). But in the spring of 2019 the other shoe dropped.

There had been a brief brouhaha when Sir Roger was appointed to be the unpaid chair of the British government's Building Better, Building Beautiful Commission. No one was more qualified for the job. But the illiberal Left came out of the woodwork screaming and yelling, and practically identified Scruton with fascism. His "cultured despisers" were the living, breathing embodiment of the culture of repudiation in its most hysterical and malicious forms. Then came the interview in the *New Statesman* with a young man, George Eaton, who set out to destroy Sir Roger's reputation. Quotations were doctored, words were taken out of context, and some alleged remarks were simply fabricated. James Brokenshire, the Tory Secretary of State for Housing, fired Sir Roger without even making an elementary effort to examine the *New Statesman's* hit job and without consulting with Roger himself. The cancel culture set out to destroy Sir Roger, once and for all. Yet letters of support came (literally) from all over the world. The conservative public intellectual Douglas Murray managed to obtain the original tapes, thus vindicating Sir Roger against calumnies which included Islamophobia, anti-Semitism, homophobia, and even hatred of the Chinese people (and not the Communist dictatorship that he deplored). Eventually Scruton was vindicated, and the *New Statesman* offered an apology. He was reinstated to the government commission from which he had been so unceremoniously sacked. The cowardice of the mainstream Tory establishment was revealed for all to see. The latter came as a terrible blow to Sir Roger since he had defended a broadly conservative vision for Britain for a full half-century.

In the midst of this controversy then came a virulent form of cancer. Through these terrible trials, Roger kept his honor, his dignity, and his self-respect. In a 2019 diary, published in the London *Spectator*, Roger ended gracefully with an admirable expression of gratitude. He was grateful to Murray and other friends who rallied to his defense. He was grateful for the doctors who cared for him during his illness. And he was grateful to all those from around the world who rallied to his defense even as he was bitterly and unfairly maligned in the Britain he loved. But mainly he was grateful for the gift of life, whose goodness impending death reveals in full clarity. And finally, I suspect, he was grateful to the Most High for having the privilege to live as an incarnate person in a world where trust, fidelity, friendship, and beauty are great gifts and not passing and ungrounded illusions as our intellectual sophisticates so dogmatically and falsely claim.

I am grateful to Roger Scruton for everything he has taught me about civilized life and the gift that we call the soul. I will miss his books, coming out one or two or three a year, giving students and admirers of Sir Roger so much to ponder, debate, and admire. A book on Wagner's *Parsifal* followed in May 2020, shortly after his death. In that great opera, Wagner offered a model of redemption, while not Christian, that offered grace and solace to the soul. He offered the "musical equivalent of forgiveness and closure." Scruton's religious views are not reducible to Wagner's, but he found profound truth in Wagner's vision of compassion and redemption in this life. *Against the Tide*, Mark Dooley's superb collection of Scruton's journalistic writings, appeared in early 2022. And who knows? There may also be other surprises—other gifts down the line. We have many reasons to be grateful to this learned, humane, and courageous defender of the human soul and the rich inheritance that is Western civilization.

## Sources and Suggested Readings

For a fuller account of Roger Scruton's life and intellectual itinerary, see the invaluable *Conversations with Roger Scruton* conducted by Mark Dooley in March 2015 and published by Bloomsbury in 2016. Scruton's *Gentle Regrets*, published in paperback by Continuum in 2006, is indispensable for understanding Scruton's turn toward conservatism and his eventual "return to religion," the theme of the concluding chapter of the book.

On the nuanced philosophical dimensions of that return, see the searching, and sometimes splendid essays collected in James Bryon, editor,

*The Religious Philosophy of Roger Scruton* (Bloomsbury, 2016). Scruton's return to the Christian faith, however idiosyncratic, is built upon his prior philosophical recovery of the "life-world," of the "ineffable" in the aesthetic realm, and the "sacred" in which personhood, consciousness, and moral agency dwell and find their expression. On this point, see Scruton's helpful and revealing essay, "A Transcendental Argument for the Transcendental" in *The Religious Philosophy of Roger Scruton*, pp. 17–31, especially pp. 29–31. As Scruton argues in this essay, philosophical reflection can only do so much to restore a place for a religious understanding of the human condition in the contemporary world. But something, he wryly adds, is much to be preferred than the "nothing" that is on offer in the dominant currents of thought. As Mark Dooley argued quite persuasively in the pages of *The Critic* (January 12, 2021), it is pure fiction to suggest that Scruton was an atheist who defended religion for cultural or aesthetic prejudice. Dooley aptly entitled his piece, "Roger Scruton was no atheist."

## Chapter 2

# COMMUNION AND CONSENT: PIERRE MANENT ON THE WELLSPRINGS OF WESTERN LIBERTY

Let us now cross the English Channel, la Manche as the French call it. It is a great pleasure to speak about Pierre Manent's political and philosophical reflection. Pierre is not only an old and dear friend, but he is arguably the thinker who has had the greatest influence on my own intellectual itinerary. To this day, I remember discovering some of his writings in the Georgetown University library in the summer of 1984. I read the French edition of *Tocqueville and the Nature of Democracy*[1] with an acute recognition that this book was something very different from a scholarly work even of the most impressive kind. Here was an exceedingly eloquent work—some of its *aperçus* were as memorable as any Pascalian *pensée*—that not only clarified Tocqueville's intention (which is no mean feat) but that taught one how to love democracy well by loving it moderately. Pierre Manent's work gave one access not only to texts but to "the world"[2]—for Manent, textual interpretation has never been an end in itself. Here was a young man—Manent was only 33 when he published this profoundly discerning work, who taught

---

1   Pierre Manent, *Tocqueville et la nature de la démocratie* (Paris: Commentaire/Juillard, 1982). The American edition appeared as *Tocqueville and the Nature of Democracy*, Foreword by Harvey C. Mansfield, translated by John Waggoner (Lanham, MD: Rowman & Littlefield Publishers, 1996).
2   The thought that classic texts provide an unparalleled "phenomenology" of the human world is brilliantly explored in Manent, "Toward the Work and Toward the World: Claude Lefort's Machiavelli" in Manent, *Modern Liberty and Its Discontents*, edited and translated by Daniel J. Mahoney and Paul Seaton (Lanham, MD: Rowman & Littlefield, 1998), pp. 47–63.

one how to think about the world, to come to terms with "modern liberty and its discontents." I had the sense of having discovered an exegete, a thinker, a commentator, who would be a guide for many years to come. That impression was only reinforced when I shortly thereafter read extraordinary essays by Manent on Charles Péguy and Raymond Aron, respectively.[3] One had the sense of being in the company of a wise man, of someone who knew how to combine wisdom and moderation with a kind of spiritual discernment. His themes from the beginning were the city and the soul, political regimes and political forms, and I knew I was along for the ride.

Shortly after meeting Manent in the fall of 1985 in Toronto and again in Paris, I had the pleasure of working through his *Intellectual History of Liberalism*[4] and *Les libéraux*,[5] his magisterial 1,000-page commented anthology on the liberal tradition. I had never seen political philosophy and political history combined in such a fruitful or suggestive way. And for some reason, Manent and I hit it off. He was only eleven years older than I but was light-years ahead of me in his engagement with the breadth and depth of the Western tradition. Still, we had the same interests, the same heroes (Tocqueville and Aron among them), and the same desire to "conjugate" Catholicism and the tradition of political philosophy as rediscovered by Leo Strauss. It was the beginning of an enduring friendship. Over the last 37 years, this friendship has grown and become more reciprocal—I would like to believe that my own work has taught Pierre Manent a few things along the way. In any case, in this chapter I hope to provide a nonsystematic introduction to and reflection upon some of the major themes in Pierre Manent's rich and diverse corpus.

The fall of 2010 saw the publication of two remarkable books by Pierre Manent. Near the end of my presentation, I'll have more to say about the

---

3   These essays on Péguy and Aron can be found in Manent, *Enquête sur la démocratie: Études de philosophie politique* (Paris: Gallimard, 2007).

4   For an American edition, see Manent, *An Intellectual History of Liberalism*, translated by Rebecca Balinski (Princeton, NJ: Princeton University Press, 1994).

5   Manent, *Les Libéraux* (Paris: Gallimard/Tel, 2001). This remarkable anthology, originally published in 1986, covers the full range of the liberal tradition, with accompanying insights on political history, from Milton and Locke to Hayek and de Jouvenel.

second of these two books, *Les métamorphoses de la cité: Essai sur la dynamique de l'occident*,[6] translated into English by Marc A. LePain as *Metamorphoses of the City: On the Western Dynamic* (Harvard University Press, 2013). It provides a deep and comprehensive interpretation of Western civilization and the fullest and most satisfying summation of Manent's reflection on the city and the soul, philosophy and politics, political forms, and the place of the Christian proposition in the self-understanding of Western civilization. The book also corrects what Manent now sees as his one-sided emphasis on the "modern difference" in his 1994 book *The City of Man*,[7] an equally rich work that attempted to delineate what is distinctive about modern political consciousness. For now, I want to trace some of Manent's core convictions about politics, philosophy, and religion with the help of *Le regard politique*,[8] *Seeing Things Politically*, translated by Ralph C. Hancock and published in translation by St. Augustine's Press in 2015, an insightful and instructive book of conversations with Manent that was published at the same time as *Les métamorphoses de la cité*. It will remain for some time the best entry into his thought as a whole. Its title suggests the centrality of politics for Manent. But a reader would be mistaken to confuse politics as Manent understands it, the human capacity to put reasons and actions in common, with the politicization of every aspect of life which is the hallmark of modern ideology. Such politicization is the enemy of true politics as Pierre Manent understands it.

*Seeing Things Politically* is undoubtedly Manent's most personal book. All of us—and that includes close friends and even family members—learned new things about the man and thinker from reading this work. I must confess that I read the 265 pages in the French edition in two sittings and have rarely been as moved or inspired by a book as I was in turning to this one. In a charming account, we learn about Manent's Communist youth, a perfectly happy boyhood, I should add. The young Manent took

6   Manent, *Les métamorphoses de la cité: Essai sur la dynamique de l'Occident* (Paris: Flammarion, 2010).

7   For the American edition, see Manent, *The City of Man*, translated by Marc A. LePain (Princeton, NJ: Princeton University Press, 1998).

8   Pierre Manent, *Le regard politique: Entretiens avec Bénédicte Delorme-Montini* (Paris: Flammarion, 2010).

inspiration from Soviet cosmonauts and believed in the promise of revolution and the classics of Marxist-Leninism until he was sixteen or so. An
American can't quite imagine being an ex-Communist at seventeen! But
we should not forget that Manent was raised in an atmosphere that can
only be described as ideologically uniform. His work makes much of conversion, of the turning of the soul to the call which is truth. It is for him
the central act which defines the West as a civilization, a possibility which
is denied at the cost of the soul's integrity and our civilization's vitality. Manent is in fact a double convert. His first conversion was to an unsentimen-
tal Catholicism, a conversion that was influenced and made possible by his
high school teacher Louis Jugnet, a Thomist of the old school. Manent did
not have a "road to Damascus experience," nor did emotion play a major
role in his conversion to the Church of Rome. He had concluded that
Christianity "knew the truth about man," that the Christian proposition
gave the fullest and most complete account of the human condition and
the nature of things. That is one of the first things to observe about Pierre
Manent: his affirmation of Christianity is never at the expense of reason
and has nothing to do with fideism, emotivism, or sentimentality. In *Seeing
Things Politically*, he tells us that his life and work exist in relation to the
three great "poles of human existence," politics, philosophy, and religion,
and he is determined to do justice to all three sides of the triangle.[9]

His second conversion was to a robust form of political reason, a
human possibility represented, above all, by the great French political
thinker Raymond Aron (1905–1983). In *Seeing Things Politically*, Manent
does not hesitate to compare Aron to Cicero, another one of Manent's intellectual heroes. He has in mind the political Cicero, far more than the
author of the *Republic* and the *Laws*. Aron, like the political Cicero, was an
"orator" who spoke and wrote "with authority and competence and eloquence on public affairs."[10] Manent reminds us of the rarity and grandeur
of such men: Ciceros, Burkes, and Arons do not come along every day;
they are, in fact, much rarer than great men of science and are almost always
underestimated.[11] While flashy Parisian intellectuals such as Sartre justified

9   Manent, *Seeing Things Politically*, pp. 59–60.
10  Ibid., p. 37.
11  Ibid.

terror and tyranny in the name of philosophy and human "emancipation," shamelessly apologizing for Soviet, Maoist, and Castroite despotisms, Aron courageously defended the reason and moderation which are integral to free political life. Aron is sometimes mistakenly seen as a skeptic. In fact, he could not abide the *nihilism* undergirding the irresponsibility and "fellow-traveling" of intellectuals. Manent's conversion to Aron and political reason was, of course, also a turn away from Communism, that deadly enemy in the twentieth century of liberty and human dignity. There was no doubt a division of labor among Aron's friends and disciples, and Manent has never specialized in the study of totalitarianism in the manner of his friend Alain Besançon. But one only has to read his treatment of Communism and National Socialism in *A World Beyond Politics?* to see the depth of his understanding of the two totalitarian scourges that competed for the souls of Western man and were the deadliest enemies that Western civilization had ever known.[12] We will return to that treatment later in this book.

If both Christianity and Aron played crucial roles in shaping Manent's intellectual orientation, the encounter with Leo Strauss was no less fundamental.[13] But in this case, it would be wrong to speak of a conversion. Just as Jugnet had pointed Manent to Aron, Aron recommended that Manent read Strauss to address some of Manent's perplexities regarding modernity and political philosophy. But the metaphorical passing of the baton did not mean that Manent was leaving Christianity and Aron's model of political reason behind. He continued to believe that Christianity "knew the truth about man" even as Aron turned him "definitively toward political things as the site where human life finds its proper tension and reveals its stakes."[14] At the same time, Manent tells us he desired some "measure," some "transcendent measure,"[15] that would make it possible to understand and regulate life. Aron, while by no means hostile to religion or the spirit of classical political philosophy, was more satisfied with the morality that was imminent

---

12  See the penetrating analyses of totalitarianism ("The Question of Communism" and "Is There a Nazi Mystery?") in Manent, *A World beyond Politics? A Defense of the Nation-State*, translated by Marc A. LePain (Princeton, NJ: Princeton University Press, 2006), pp. 151–70.

13  See *Seeing Things Politically*, pp. 38–39.

14  Ibid., p. 38.

15  Ibid., p. 39.

in human and political life. He was in some sense, Manent argues, "the perfect gentleman."[16] In contrast, Strauss, the German émigré, the author of *Natural Right and History*, provided a more radical critique of the modern insistence that thought was determined by society. His anti-historicism and his doubts about the modern project appealed to Manent, even as Manent wrestled with Strauss's claim that philosophy and religion were two noble if incompatible ways of life, ways of life that could be "synthesized" only at the expense of the integrity of both.

Manent tells us that he continued to wander and hesitate between "the equilibrium and the beautiful architecture of Thomism and Strauss's austere demand that (he) choose between philosophy and religion."[17] To that extent, Manent remains on the edge of the Straussian family, more a Straussian fellow-traveler than a Straussian, since he rejects Strauss's claim that one must finally choose between philosophy and faith. He sees himself as being inside the triangle formed by politics, philosophy, and religion, refusing "complete devotion"[18] to any one of the poles. A critic might be tempted to say that this refusal risks making Manent a tepid believer as well as a bad Straussian! But in truth, what motivates Manent is fidelity to experience in all its amplitude. He refuses all thoughtless syntheses but also an account of the philosophic life that makes the philosopher into something other than a human being. He refuses to accept a too radical, even inhuman, separation between philosophy and religion, or the intellectual and moral virtues. In *Metamorphoses of the City*, Manent ends his long treatment of Augustine's *The City of God* by creating a dialogue between St. Augustine and Strauss on precisely these questions.[19] He sides with Augustine while giving Strauss his due. Let us turn briefly to this text to illustrate one of the ways Manent navigates the three great poles of human existence.

Manent begins his discussion by noting that for St. Augustine,

16  Ibid.
17  Ibid., p. 46.
18  Ibid., p. 59.
19  Manent, *Metamorphoses of the City*, pp. 293–95. Manent broadens the dialogue, with the help of Pascal, in "Between Athens and Jerusalem," *First Things* (February 2012). In that piece, Manent emphasizes that Christianity never loses its "dialectical" dependence on the Jewish people or Greek philosophical wisdom.

Christianity incorporates and overcomes two "ruptures" within humanity that are also "decisive pieces of qualitative progress in the self-consciousness of humanity": the rupture or separation between the Jews, "the chosen people" and the "nations," on the one hand, and the Greek separation between the philosopher and the ordinary person, which builds upon a more primordial separation between the soul and the body, on the other.[20] For Augustine, Christianity confirms these two separations while overcoming them: "the mediation of the God-man Christ" allows unity to be reestablished on a higher level. Manent succinctly summarizes a profound Augustinian insight: "Augustine's presentation makes Christianity appear as the resolution of the most profound and fruitful fractures of human unity: the Jewish and the Greek."[21]

But following Strauss, Manent then "rotates the triangle"[22] to allow us to look at Christianity from the point of view of the Jewish law and Greek philosophy. From these perspectives, the Christian "synthesis" of Jewish law and Greek philosophy weakens or mixes up "what is most 'interesting' in each of the two elements." "Christianity then appears as the tempting but disappointing mixture of a law that does not truly command and a philosophy that does not truly seek."[23] If that were the final word, Manent would side with the Straussian critique of Christianity for "mixing up" that which can only be properly understood in isolation and opposition.

But Manent does not stop here. He presents an Augustinian response to Strauss. He acknowledges what he succinctly calls "the mystery of election," the mystery of God's chosen people. He also acknowledges the truth in the classical insight that only a small number of truly "wise" men are capable of being philosophers. He—and his Augustine—are willing to grant Strauss all that. Still, Manent's Augustine, and in these passages Augustine is clearly speaking for Manent (or is it the other way around?), insists that to reject the Christian synthesis is "to accept two 'separations' against which something in the human being can only protest."[24] In Manent's view, the

20  Ibid., pp. 294.
21  Ibid.
22  Ibid.
23  Ibid.
24  Ibid., p. 295.

unity of man under the God-man Christ can preserve separations: it is in truth the modern "religion of humanity" that extends the law—or rights—to all humans in the name of an indiscriminate egalitarianism. Christianity preserves the special place for the Jews as well as the Platonic discovery of the conceptual distinction between the body and the soul. Rather than being a synthesis that obliterates "separations," Christianity is best understood as a middle way, a truthful mean, between Greek and Jewish separations, and the "maximum synthesis" of the Moderns, a synthesis that does away with all ruptures and mediations.[25] It is fair to say that something in Pierre Manent's soul cries out—discreetly to be sure!—against a conception of the philosopher who is trans-moral, trans-religious, and in decisive respects, trans-human. Paradoxically, such a view has no place for a genuine "transcendent measure," one that does justice to the proximity of human experience to a divine ground of existence. For all his debts to Strauss, Manent does not conceive philosophy in the Straussian manner or accept the separations made possible by Greek philosophy or the Jewish law as the final word on the human condition.

But if Pierre Manent vindicates the Christian conjugation of unity and separation against both the Straussian critique and the modern effacement of hierarchy and distinction, he at the same time does not hesitate to confront what he perceives as a gaping political deficit at the heart of Christianity. Manent is with Pascal in affirming that the Christian religion "has well understood mankind."[26] At the same time, he expresses doubts about the ability of Christianity to translate that understanding into an account of the human condition that can do justice to the political nature of man. The Christian temptation is to "despise the temporal,"[27] as the great French Catholic poet and philosopher Charles Péguy put it, to treat human beings as already having been transformed by the perfection that belongs to the kingdom of heaven alone. The pagan virtues—honor, courage, confidence

25  Ibid.
26  *Seeing Things Politically*, p. 62.
27  See Pierre Manent, "Libéral et Catholique" in *Penser le monde moderne: Le bon grain et l'ivraie* sous la direction de Philippe Bénéton et Marie-Jeanne Seppey (Paris: Editions Cujas, 2009), pp. 7–11. This brief but penetrating essay explains why it is a mistake for Christians to disdain the liberal order despite its obvious imperfections and limitations.

in the human capacity to govern oneself in freedom—have been distrusted by Christians who are tempted to see the natural order as already having been definitively transformed by grace. Not only is Christianity in tension with the legitimate pride, the self-respect and confidence in one's forces that allows human beings to live in freedom, but it has difficulty giving a persuasive account of human experience on its own terms. The temptation to despise the world has given rise to quasi-utopian political options beloved by both the Christian Left and Right: mythical "Third Ways," authoritarian corporatist states, dreams of socialism that will somehow dispense with violence and coercion. Sins that are coextensive with the human condition are attributed to a liberal order which, for better or worse, is the "temporal order" of the modern world.[28] Manent is one of those rare thinkers who neither genuflects before the modern liberal order or denies the considerable goods—civic peace, prosperity and dignity for masses of human beings, religious liberty—to which it has given rise. In Manent's view, there is a "noble risk" in accepting our liberal "temporal order" and bringing Christian conscience and classical wisdom to bear in humanizing and elevating it.

But if Christians have difficulty "thinking politically," a point stressed by Christianity's most polemical opponents, such as Machiavelli and Rousseau, it has a more fundamental difficulty remaining "faithful to human experience."[29] The language of piety often covers over tensions between body and soul, nature and law, faith and reason that constitute the human condition. As Manent bluntly puts it in *Seeing Things Politically*: "[W]e have to admit that religious people sometimes lack certain scruples where experiential truth is concerned when they propose an understanding of humanity already pre-treated for the uses they have in mind. In such cases, the Answer has smothered the questions."[30] He adds that "a work that satisfactorily brings together fidelity to human experience and commitment to a religious perspective is rare,"[31] indeed. Yet in a beautiful discussion in *Seeing Things Politically*, he adds that there is one great book

28  Ibid., pp. 10–11.
29  *Seeing Things Politically*, p. 63.
30  Ibid., pp. 62–63.
31  Ibid. p. 63.

where the two are "strangely, paradoxically reconciled."[32] That book is the Bible. In that work, one finds "at once, directly and immediately, human experience in its greatest ignorance of God and, mysteriously, a presence of God that does not impinge upon, that does not cover up the authenticity of experience."[33] In the *Psalms* in particular, Manent finds "an experience of something radically different from all human experience but which does not prevent this experience from being lived and described in its whole truth, in its nakedness."[34] He does not hesitate to suggest that this ability to hold together "what no human being can hold together within the limits of human expression" is an argument for the Bible's "revealed character."[35]

What we find in Manent's work is a vindication of the Christian proposition that owes little or nothing to the defensiveness or evasiveness (and one might say "bad faith") sometimes characteristic of the "party of the Church." Contemporary Christians have a hard time supporting or endorsing a liberal democratic order unless that order is somehow perceived as the "secularization" of Christian wisdom itself. Many serious Christians find the distant origins of the liberal and democratic dispensation in the Middle Ages, in the Gospels, anywhere but in the anti-Christian polemics of the philosophical architects of the modern project. The Catholic Church used to see in modern democracy a secular revolt against the authority of God, an unleashing of human willfulness; now it sees in the rights of man the working out of a conception of human dignity whose ultimate roots lie in the Gospels themselves.[36]

Manent's work points in a different direction. He is deeply and profoundly critical of the "willfulness" inherent in the modern project. The Church was right to see in the "religion of humanity," in the self-deification of man, its deadliest enemy. At the same time, Manent argues that republican liberty, with its confidence in man's ability to govern itself, is by no means incompatible with an affirmation of ontological and political limits. The

32  Ibid.
33  Ibid.
34  Ibid.
35  Ibid.
36  See Manent, "Christianity and Democracy: Some Remarks on the Political History of Religion, or, on the Religious History of Modern Politics" in Manent, *Modern Liberty and Its Discontents*, pp. 97–115, esp. pp. 97–104.

dialectic of magnanimity and humility has marked the West from the beginning and continues to operate, however dimly, within our liberal dispensation. The liberal state allows human beings to govern themselves better than they were governed during the long Middle Ages, not to mention under the authoritarian corporatist states in Austria or Portugal upon which the Catholic Church looked with some favor in the years before World War II.[37] Today, the Church can play its role in reminding the citizens of modern democracies that liberty must bow to truth if our freedom is to be worthy of human beings. This is the "dialectical advantage"[38] which Christianity holds under a liberal order—the Church has *something to say* about the nature and needs of human beings and ends and purposes of human freedom.[39] Moreover, liberal freedom needs the guidance of conscience, that great internal tribunal which points to a measure or standard of judgment above the human will.[40] Conscience ceases to be itself when it succumbs to the subjectivist temptation, when it is closed to the intrusion of all authoritative institutions and truth claims. The Christian proposition thus reminds liberalism of the goods of life that it is tempted to leave behind in its rush to reject every form of "heteronomous" domination. But Manent reminds us that there are "deep waters" underlying our thin—our all-too-thin—affirmation of individual autonomy: Modern rights cannot so easily escape the demands or requirements of Christian conscience or the moral authority of heroes and saints. Manent shows us that it takes great forbearance, unrivaled spiritual maturity and political moderation and wisdom to avoid the twin temptations of Progress and Reaction, both of which are forms of "despising the temporal." Manent's position is subtle and demanding enough that at various times it has been confused with a visceral anti-modernism and with a Catholicism that has made fatal compromises with philosophical liberalism. It is hard to understand and appreciate the *juste milieu.*

One of Pierre Manent's fundamental insights is that it is impossible for human beings to live long or well outside the framework of collective life

---

37  *Seeing Things Politically*, pp. 169–70.
38  See Manent, "Christianity and Democracy" in *Modern Liberty and Its Discontents*, p. 115.
39  Ibid., pp 112–15.
40  *Seeing Things Politically*, pp. 168–69.

that he calls the "political form."[41] His work provides a remarkable encapsulation of the "finite" number of political forms—tribe, city, nation, empire—that are available to human beings.[42] Today, Manent suggests, Europeans attempt to escape the demands of national life without establishing a truly sovereign body that will take the place of the nation as the frame or form of political life. This post-national or post-political democracy made possible by the European project in its present form replaces politics with a non-negotiable *règle*—a rule-based society dominated by administrative or bureaucratic dictates[43]—that always and everywhere have priority over the will of the people as expressed in democratic elections or in referenda about the future of the European community. With an eye to the alleged inevitability of ever greater European integration and territorial expansion, Manent has spoken of a *kratos* without a *demos*,[44] a particularly suggestive way of highlighting what political scientists more typically call Europe's "democratic deficit." In *Seeing Things Politically*, Manent provocatively refers to a "European vacation"[45] made possible by American power and by the deluded European belief that its abdication of political responsibility somehow makes it the *avant garde* of humanity. But Manent points out that "the large national and religious associations"[46] of the world—the United States first and foremost, but also China, Russia, the Islamic world, and aspiring powers such as India and Brazil—do not share Europe's post-political illusion. They do not confuse globalization, the very palpable global network of commerce, trade, and communications, with the political and spiritual unification of mankind. Europeans are, Manent suggests, under the spell of a religious or quasi-religious ideal which is impervious

---

41    See Manent, "The Question of Political Forms" in *A World beyond Politics?*, pp. 42–50 and the sketch of the "history of political forms" provided in *Le regard politique*, pp. 147–49.

42    *Seeing Things Politically*, pp. 116–18.

43    *Seeing Things Politically*, p. 156.

44    Manent, *Democracy Without Nations?: The Fate of Self-Government in Europe*, translated by Paul Seaton (Wilmington, DE: ISI Books, 2007), p. 7. This work is an augmented American edition of *La raison des nations: Réflexions sur la démocratie en Europe* (Paris: Gallimard, 2006).

45    *Seeing Things Politically*, p. 146.

46    Ibid., p. 151.

to all evidence that suggests that human beings remain "political animals" and that democracy needs a body or framework—a "political form"—to give it life. Manent calls this illusion "the religion of humanity" (this religion was literally invented by the French philosopher and sociologist Auguste Comte in the 1830s but it has deep roots in the emphasis on human self-sovereignty which is coextensive with modern political philosophy), a religion that also aims to replace the old common morality of Europe with a democratic sentimentality, a humanitarianism, that is more abstract and less demanding than the old-fashioned love of neighbor. In Manent's view, it is a mistake to confuse this abstract religion of humanity with the common good, with the great task of "putting things in common" which has been central to European and Western life for the past two and a half millennia, or with the Christian proposition, rightly understood.

In a series of books and essays, Manent has criticized the reduction of life and politics to the single imperative of choice or democratic consent. In his 1996 essay, "Democracy Without Nations?," he points out the limits of submitting "all aspects of the world to a single principle,"[47] even if that principle is liberty itself. Manent insists that even liberty, the modern "value" par excellence, has need of limits. First and foremost among these limits is the political body that allows a community of free men and women to "put things in common" and to relate itself to a broader framework of time and space. Without such self-limitation, the principle of consent risks becoming a principle of "political impotence and paralysis"[48] when it becomes identified with a pure abstraction. "Pure democracy" lacks a proper sense of continuity with the past, with the national framework that gave rise to democracy in the first place, and at the same time runs roughshod over the expressed democratic will of the people. One saw the undemocratic character of "pure democracy" at work in 2005 when the European elite responded to "No" votes on the European constitution in France and the Netherlands by arbitrarily transforming the rejected constitution into the Treaty of Lisbon, a treaty which would not need popular consent to be

---

47  This essay appears as an Appendix to Manent, *Democracy Without Nations: The Fate of Self-Government in Europe*, pp. 71–86. The quotation can be found on p. 83.

48  Ibid., p. 84.

ratified. The European project so defined risks culminating in administrative despotism and postpolitical fantasies that prevent Europeans from thinking and acting politically. The alternative to the religion of humanity, to the ideal of "pure democracy," is a self-conscious effort to recover the complex ties that bind communion, truth, and consent. This demands nothing less than an exercise in political philosophy and spiritual discernment of the first order.

In a fit of heedless ingratitude, Europeans are today tempted to repudiate the framework that still connects them to their national pasts and provides "flesh" for the democratic abstractions of the "individual" and the "people." In an important 1984 essay on the political thought of the French Catholic poet-philosopher Charles Péguy (1874–1914), Manent evokes a "fundamental aspect of the theological-political problem" that Péguy "perceived . . . with deadly intensity: there is a specific sacredness of the political order as such, of the civic community."[49] This sense of civic sacredness and "belonging" is precisely what Manent is alluding to when he speaks throughout this work of the irreplaceable role of "communion" in politics, and the enduring need to weave together communion and consent. He soberly warns his fellow Europeans that if they completely break the tissue of national time, of national belonging, these longings will take the form of illiberal separatist and religious movements, movements that will be tempted to put "communion before democracy." For what is democracy without the "common," without the cultivation of shared civic communion?

As Manent put it in his impressive 2006 essay "What Is a Nation?," present-day Europeans are in the process of losing consciousness of the nation as the mean between the "powerful localism" of the city or the region and the "imperial impulse to look toward unsubdued regions beyond the horizon." Manent attributes the age-old European desire "to strike the middle ground between the puny and the immense, the petty and the limitless"[50] to the Christian character of European nations, a Christian character

49  See Manent, "Charles Péguy: Between Political Faith and Faith" in *Modern Liberty and Its Discontents*, pp. 79–95. The quotation is from p. 94.
50  Manent's 2006 lecture "What Is a Nation?" appears as an Appendix to *Democracy Without Nations?*, pp. 87–103. See p. 103 for the quotation.

that today is more and more forgotten and under assault. According to Manent, one political consequence of Christian charity was to weaken the grasp of localism while "assuaging the vertigo of faraway domination."[51] As European nations lose sight of their Christian character (Manent insists that Europeans need not choose between the liberal or secular state and the Christian nation, a theme later developed in *Beyond Radical Secularism*) they lose the "imaginative" capacity to see in the nation the great mediator between the universal and the particular, the faraway and the local. The affinities with Roger Scruton's understanding of "territorial democracy" and critique of *oikophobia* (hatred of home) are apparent here.

This reflects one of the salient features of the religion of humanity, namely, its hostility to all mediations," to everything that gives modern democracy concreteness and life. In contrast, communion entails "putting things in common," an operation, an activity, that can never be fully achieved. The nation is the modern manifestation of community or communion, par excellence, the framework of common life (and historical continuity) that allows men and women to put things in common. But Manent points out that the "philosophy" of communion has a great epistemological disadvantage in a democratic age: while the individual with his accompanying rights is a tangible thing, something that can be seen and touched, the notion of the common seems inexact, unduly blurry or out of focus for modern men and women who prefer scientific precision to the goods of life. "The philosophy of what is common is [thus] condemned to struggle against this epistemological bias of contemporary democratic civilization."[52] To be sure, there are, indeed, tangible signs or expressions of the public thing: Public buildings, parliaments and national assemblies. But in the end the "common" is much more a task than a place, an imperative to produce "an order in which human beings can conduct their lives in the most deliberate way possible."[53] The modern social sciences, in particular economics and political science, are built on the twin poles of the individual (with his interests and rights) and the "representative" state: in the decisive respects they presuppose the "disappearance" of the common. Manent

---

51  Ibid.
52  *Seeing Things Politically*, p. 155.
53  Ibid., p. 154.

insists that the "general rule" is in no way the "common thing": "the ideal of European life [today] . . . is that we would all be governed by general rules and that all action would be subsumed under a rule, with evaluating institutions for verifying that things are done by the rules."[54] *Governance*, so understood, is diametrically opposed to *politics* where free men and women govern themselves. The "tyranny of the rule," of the rule-based society, paradoxically appeals to the principle of consent, to an abstract idea of "humanitarian" democracy, even as it crowds out the concrete manifestations of democratic life that are incompatible with the purity of the democratic ideal. At the same time, Europeans move back and forth from dogmatic egalitarianism—rooted in the religion of humanity—and the demands of economic competition. There is nothing in principle to mediate or moderate this unthinking oscillation between humanitarianism and economic necessity since "the common" has been displaced as the great "guide" and "stabilizer" of European life. The European "construction," understood as indefinite territorial expansion under the allegedly benign supervision of Brussels, persists as the alpha and omega of contemporary European life.[55] Nothing, certainly not the democratic will of peoples, will be allowed to get in its way. Despite its malaise, a "depoliticized" Europe takes comfort in its moral superiority to all those peoples (in truth, the rest of humanity) who do not yet acknowledge the wisdom of leaving History behind. A "vacation," an abdication of responsibilities, is thus confused with an ascent to a higher level of humanity.

One can contrast this European "vacation," this abdication of political responsibility, this absence of any serious reflection on political forms, with the confidence in mankind's ability to act which formed the life blood of the West for two and a half millennia. In *Metamorphoses of the City*, Manent argues that the greatest revolution in the Western world was not the modern project that gave rise to science, liberalism, and democracy, but rather that first great "putting in common" which was the Greek city.[56] In traditional tribal or patriarchal orders, human action was constricted and was frowned upon as a crime or transgression against the order of the gods. The city gave

54  Ibid., p. 156.
55  Ibid., p. 187.
56  *Metamorphoses of the City*, p. 4.

human beings confidence in their own powers and rendered them capable of acting. The Greek city was not the product of a project, but it was in the city that men first learned how to govern themselves. In the city, the Greeks "discover[ed] and learn[ed] politics, which is the great domain of [human] action."[57] The modern project did not entail, at least initially, the founding of a radically distinct human order but rather a *political* project which responded to Europe's "theological-political problem."[58] Instead of beginning with the "modern difference," as he had in works such as *The City of Man*, Manent now attempts to place the modern project in the broader history of the Western or European political development. Modern "constructivism" presupposed and built upon a prior confidence in the human capacity to act.[59] During what Manent calls Europe's long "Ciceronian moment," when European thought and action had been torn by the conflicting claims and authority of the city, empire, and Church, the capacity to act had been stifled. Europeans lived under "mixed" authorities and the concurrence of these forms of association produced what Manent calls an "awful disorder."[60]

This quarrel about political forms was a quarrel about much more than institutions. Most profoundly, it was a quarrel about the human type that ought to inspire European life. As Manent eloquently puts it in the "Introduction" to *Metamorphoses of the City*, "Who was one to imitate? Was it necessary to follow the life of humble sacrifice of which Christ furnishes the model? Or was it necessary to lead the active and proud life of the citizen warrior of which Rome was the framework and the product *par excellence*? And among the pagans themselves, should we admire Cato, or rather Caesar?" Manent tellingly adds that "Europeans did not know which city they wanted to or could inhabit; they did not know which man they wanted to or could be."[61] The modern project arose precisely from this "radical perplexity."[62] Manent shows how both the Reformation and Machiavelli

57  Ibid., p. 4.
58  Ibid., pp. 6–9.
59  Ibid., pp. 1–14.
60  Ibid., p. 6.
61  Ibid.
62  Ibid.

attempted to redress this "overabundance" of political forms and human types.[63] The disjunction or tension between speech and action in the European Christian world was first navigated by the national form and the Christian or confessional state "which preceded and conditioned the [modern] representative regime."[64] But today, post-political Europeans confront not an overabundance but a "dearth" of political forms: "the civic operation is anesthetized and the religious speech nearly inaudible."[65]

I must confess that I am as convinced by the earlier Manentian arguments and analyses as I am by his more recent, subtle, dialectical self-correction. Is not the anesthetization of the European capacity for a *production du commun*, the bringing together of thought and action in a truly common world open to all the contents of life, another word for Tocqueville's "democratic revolution," if not a radicalization of that revolution of which Tocqueville provides the most exact description? Perhaps a metamorphosis can erode the entity, in this case the West, undergoing a transformation? Manent's analysis certainly suggests as much. In any case, Pierre Manent is right that we must finally understand modernity from a perspective that is neither "modern" nor "anti-modern." That is the task of equitable or balanced analysis. Instructed by Manent, we are obliged to open ourselves to the "metamorphoses of the city," to that initial and prodigious putting of human things in common if we are to find our way again. Pierre Manent helps all of us, and that includes Americans who sometimes forget we are the heirs and caretakers of European civilization, to understand our profound debt to the plural civilization which was the West. It would be premature, it would show an absence of confidence in our own forces, to suppose that the Western adventure is over.

63   Ibid., pp. 7–10 and pp. 310–23.
64   Ibid., pp. 9–10.
65   Ibid., p. 10.

# Chapter 3
# 1968, FRENCH LIBERAL CONSERVATISM, AND THE PHILOSOPHICAL RESTORATION OF LIBERTY UNDER LAW

Roger Scruton long argued that French intellectual life was taken over by "imposters" in the 1960s. There is much evidence to support his claim. As we have already noted, Jean-Paul Sartre's political commitments were perverse and even imbecilic—this talented *philosophe* and *littérateur* defended the most vile tyrannies as long as they were left-wing. He saw authenticity and emancipation at work in Stalin's murderous despotism, Castro's brutal Caribbean tyranny, and Mao's terroristic assault on human freedom and the life of the mind. Most perversely of all, in the *Critique of Dialectical Reason* (1960), he provided a "philosophical" defense of "fraternity terror" as a means of overcoming inauthenticity and bourgeois individualism. The radical existentialist could only find fleeting moments of hope in the bloodlust of revolutionary terror, heads on pikes and the "joy of the (revolutionary) knife." Scruton rightly calls Sartre's political choices and judgments "degraded," owing as much to Robespierre as Marx, although certainly indebted to both.

But Sartre was a writer of talent and a keen, if one-sided, observer of the human condition when he was not deformed by ideology. The same cannot be said of true phonies like Louis Althusser who, Scruton argues, degraded both political judgment and the very possibility of a thoughtful encounter with our humanity. "Structuralist" Marxism, à la Althusser, was not even particularly faithful to the Marxism of Marx. The Paris "nonsense machine," as Scruton bitingly calls it, was committed to a reckless assault on common sense, moderation, and decency. In addition, it displayed fierce hostility to even a residual conception of a (normative) human nature. To be sure, Michel Foucault had his moments of genius. But he shared, and radicalized, his generation's obsession with sex and power relations, seeing domination everywhere, except in Tehran (in 1979) and in Mao's China, where he perversely discerned avatars of liberation.

As for Deleuze, Lacan, and the rest, they synthesized Marx, Freud, and contemporary nihilism ("poststructuralism") in an obscurantist mix that will always remain inaccessible to the uninitiated. In their hands, thought was transformed into an instrument of pure destruction, so-called "deconstruction," at the service of what Scruton so memorably labelled "the culture of repudiation." Like the Russian nihilists of old, the representatives of cultural repudiation set out to destroy the remnants of the natural moral law and all authoritative institutions necessary to free and civilized life. Today, Alain Badiou is their self-parodic heir. This French "philosopher" combines secular messianic effusions about "the Event," an eruption of revolutionary bliss and destruction, with apologies for Stalin and Mao. In the Chinese tyrant's violent discourses during the murderous Cultural Revolution, Badiou finds the voice of philosophy at the service of the world-transforming Event. For many in the Western intellectual world, these figures are the only intellectual France they know. Sophisticated nihilism is lauded by academics and literati throughout the world.

But there is "another aspect of French intellectual life," as Scruton well observes. For example, the French political thinker Raymond Aron combined immense learning with manly sobriety and measured political judgment. He famously resisted the totalitarian temptation in all its forms. In the present cultural moment, when communism again appeals to the militants (and some of the tender-hearted) in the new generation, Aron's *The Opium of the Intellectuals* (1955, 1957 for the English-language edition) remains a powerful guide to intellectual and moral hygiene. Unfortunately, in France today, many pay lip service to Aron's anti-totalitarianism while ignoring, or at least downplaying, his equally bold and outspoken resistance to everything associated with the "thought of 1968."

The old and distinguished Parisian publisher Calmann-Lévy recently reissued Aron's *La révolution introuvable* (*The Elusive Revolution*), which attacked both the rather juvenile Castroism and Maoism of the soixante-huitards while diagnosing their pathological appeal to a radical individualism, a moral antinomianism, which took aim at the very idea of ordered or structured liberty. The new edition of the book is introduced by Philippe Raynaud, a thoughtful and wide-ranging political scientist, who today takes his bearings from a centrism of the Macron type. Without getting anything wrong per se, Raynaud's new introduction to Aron's book is a pre-eminent example of what the Hungarian philosopher Aurel Kolnai called "misplaced emphasis." Raynaud spends more time emphasizing Aron's occasional criticism of de Gaulle's government, and his calls for reform of an overly centralized French university system, than he does his bold, and truly essential, assault on the spirit of 1968 and all its works. Raynaud fails to sufficiently appreciate the prescient, even prophetic, character, of the book. Aron foresaw the culture of repudiation in all its amplitude. He was alarmed by what he eventually came to see less as a "psychodrama" (as he called it in May-June 1968) and more as a "crisis of civilization," as André Malraux called it at the time. Many "centrist" Aronians in France, Raynaud among them, prefer to ignore or downplay the Aron who emerged from the events of 1968. An indefatigable defender of the liberal university and the first great scourge of political correctness in France, Aron came to see "democratic conservatism" as essential to the preservation of civilized liberty. Here was a liberalism that knew how to "conserve."

## Aron's Critique of the New Antinomianism

This was Aron at his wisest, in command of all his powers, and hardly a cranky old man who was unwilling to accommodate what was legitimate in the "spirit of the times." Right Aronians, such as Giulio de Ligio and the eminent political philosophers Pierre Manent and Philippe Bénéton (and myself, I might add), worry less about "populism" (which has, to be sure, excesses all its own) than the accommodation of a flaccid center to the "depoliticization" of Europe and the West. That accommodating centrism is all too willing to resign itself (not enthusiastically, to be sure) to the institutionalization of the new morality and of a liberty that has little place for robust non-relativistic moral judgment.

The distinguished sociologist Dominique Schnapper, Aron's daughter, has written several excellent books about the links between democratic citizenship and a vigorous and self-respecting nation-state. She has also renewed her father's reflections on the corruption of democracy by what Montesquieu called "extreme equality." That corruption is evident when democracy rejects all authoritative institutions, and even the authority of truth itself. I particularly recommend Schnapper's *Community of Citizens* and *The Democratic Spirit of Law*. In these works, one sees the best social science united to Aronian sobriety, rejecting both radical relativism and a scholarship at the service of reckless activism. But it is clear that, today, Schnapper fears the populist Right more than "the fanaticism of a center" (the phrase is Pierre Manent's) that has also said adieu to the old Aronian and Tocquevillian synthesis of liberalism and conservatism. These are matters of judgment, of course. In any case, Schnapper is more of a "sociologist" than her father and perhaps has less confidence than he did in the enduring wellsprings of human nature. In a spirit of resignation, she seems to believe that the democratic revolution, radicalized by late modernity, is destined to have the final word. In this view, the old goods can hardly be credibly renewed, or at least not anytime soon. But to Schnapper's great credit, she readily acknowledges that the morality upheld by the Catholic Church was largely the same morality upheld by the French republican tradition. She is thus no cheerleader for a secularism that wishes the Church ill or takes satisfaction from its current travails.

But nothing seems more necessary at present than the renewal of the spirit of Aron during the final fifteen years of his life, a renewal present in a genuine if austere way in Schnapper's best books. When Aron's model of spiritedness and sober realism is too readily dismissed, Aron becomes less threatening, more "democratic" and more tame. But he is, at the same time, effectively relegated to the past, to a twentieth-century struggle against communism and Nazism that is seen as of little relevance to the issues of our time. I beg to differ. At a time when a man of great intellectual integrity such as the French public philosopher Alain Finkielkraut is transformed into a diabolic figure by those who hate Israel and enforce the new political correctness, when Zionism is identified by influential currents with Nazism, when European democracy has turned against itself in a display of masochistic guilt (as if free, humane, and prosperous liberal Europe is the uniquely "culpable" civilization in all of human history), it is time to reclaim the sober and spirited civic courage of Aron.

Contemporary voices on the harder Right such as Eric Zémmour denounce progressivism, Islamism, and political correctness with a fiery gusto. They are not wrong to see a new totalitarianism springing from a cultural stance that sees in the West nothing but guilt and endless oppression. "Human rights universalism," as Zémmour calls it, attacks decent societies and bans the criticism of movements, such as radicalized political Islam, that have no place for law, moderation, or human rights. But the erudite Zémmour is more angry than thoughtful, and aims to condemn more than convince. What is truly needed today is a judicious coming together of spiritedness and moderation, liberalism (traditionally understood) and democratic conservatism, a respect for moral decency and high intellectual culture tied to the capacity for modest, non-masochistic self-criticism. That is the spirit necessary for civilizational renewal. Aron had those strengths and virtues in spades. In his final lecture at the Collège de France in 1978, *Liberté et égalité*, recently edited by and published by Pierre Manent and Giulio de Ligio, under the auspices of Dominique Schnapper, we can find a lucid précis of Aron's humane democratic conservatism at work. Let me provide a brief overview.

In that little work, Aron pointed out that the French renewal of political liberalism of the 1970s was more negative than positive, drawing almost exclusively on opposition to totalitarianism (inspired, it should be pointed out, in no small part by a partial appropriation of Aron and Solzhenitsyn). Liberalism had come to define itself by opposition to "absolutism," to every monistic appeal to absolute truth. This was part of the story but only part of it. Liberalism had been vindicated by historical experience, as a humane and viable alternative to the "absolutism of ideology." But Aron appreciated that liberalism could not be reduced to an "ideology of the rights of man," an anti-political perspective which ignored the requirements of civic virtue and civic cohesion to a political order as such. In this essay, Aron continues his dialectical reflection on the relationship between formal liberty and the ever more insistent egalitarian claims that liberty be made more real and less formal. But Aron came to see doctrinaire egalitarianism as the enemy of liberty rightly understood: liberty as equal rights could never be reduced to some impossible dream of "equal powers and capacities." As Aron put it, one can in principle give everyone access to the university system, as France had wisely or unwisely done. But one could not reasonably guarantee that all will have the same success in pursuing their studies. Extreme egalitarianism risked contradicting the deepest wellsprings of human nature and social life. It creates false hopes and grave disappointments.

Writing in 1978, Aron saw that the fierce but superficial Maoism and Castroism of the *soixante-huitards* had given way to moral anarchism and facile antinomianism. According to the thought of 1968, vastly over-represented in the academy and Western intellectual life, free societies were nothing but vehicles of limitless domination, what Roger Scruton so suggestively called the "heresy of domination." In liberal freedoms, formal but real, the new antinomians could see only unjust privilege and power at work. The hierarchies and systems of authority that belong to every social institution worthy of the name were now identified with despotism. The essential difference between liberal democracy and totalitarianism was erased at a stroke. Instead of renewing political philosophy's search for the good society or the best regime, the heirs of 1968 succumbed to what Aron called the "total refusal of existing society." If such angry moralism is not capable of a political articulation, then it is not an approach to social life that political actors, faced with concrete choices and dilemmas, can take seriously. Utopian perfection had given way to indignation and nihilistic despair. Liberation risked forging new chains.

Aron reminded *soi-disant* liberals that civic-mindedness, or political responsibility, "is part of morality." Reason, practical or political reason, should be the "star and compass," as John Locke put it, of free and responsible men and women. Practical reason demands self-command, while the new antinomianism confuses liberty with the liberation of the desires. But a hedonistic society can see in governing institutions of all stripes—civic, religious, educational, business enterprises, and the Churches and army, of course—only prohibitions that are incompatible with liberty as untethered and untutored desire. Echoing Kant, Aristotle, Montesquieu, and Tocqueville, that is to say, the best of ancient and modern wisdom, Aron eloquently defended liberty under law and freedom inescapably tied to civic self-restraint. He did so as a public philosopher, and not in the manner of a metaphysician or academic political theorist. Like Cicero of old he was a sturdy defender of the mix of civicism and morality that keeps decadence, vulgar relativism, and Epicureanism at bay.

Aron's instincts were thoroughly decent, and his liberalism thus never lost sight of the best conservative wisdom. He was not a religious man, but he respected transcendental religion and shared its solicitude for the human soul. And he was a Jew out of self-respect in an age of murderous anti-Semitism and the totalitarian degradation of the human spirit.

Near the end of *Liberté et égalité*, Aron suggests that democracies must recover a thoughtful understanding of the place of virtue in civic and moral life. Evoking Freud at his sober best, Aron defends the "reality principle" against the "pleasure principle," the unleashing or liberation of sexual eros or desire as ends in themselves. Emancipated from moral and civic superintendence, they corrode both responsible individuality and the common good of a free society. Authentic theories of liberalism and democracy must give serious reflection to the definition of the virtuous citizen in relation to the ideal of a free society. Arguments such as these help us understand why Pierre Manent has suggestively called Aron a "liberal classic" rather than a "classical liberal," in his introduction to Aron's book. Where many see the dominant influence of Max Weber's social science and Kant's moral vision in Aron's political philosophy, Manent hears an Aristotelian voice where morality and civicism come together through the mediation of the high art of political prudence. Of course, Manent acknowledges the role of all these influences in the formation of Aron's singular and still remarkably relevant conservative or restrained liberalism.

The *avant garde* of contemporary Western societies, from London and Paris to New York and Los Angeles, has made a fetish of (groundless) consent or choice. Here Aron departs in a significant way from the corruption of liberalism that has hijacked that name. Aron concedes that he shares the ideal that each individual should be free to choose his own path in life. Despite his early flirtation with Weber's radical relativism, Aron came to see that choice could never be totally free or unencumbered. Liberty is always liberty under law, or it ceases to do justice to the nature of man and society. A free, decent, and stable democratic order should never confuse the freedom to choose one's way in life with a radical relativism that gives us permission to choose our "own conceptions of good and evil." Here, Aron would and could not go. Good and evil, he argued, are available to decent men and women who see things as they come to sight in ordinary experience. Tyranny is not "monarchy misliked," as Thomas Hobbes famously quipped in *Leviathan*. It always and everywhere entails an assault on the bodies and souls of human beings. In his eminently practical way, Aron affirmed and lived the cardinal virtues so dear to Aristotle and Cicero: prudence, courage, temperance, and justice. He brought classical moderation to bear on modern liberty.

In the last years of his life, Aron gave much thought to the need to teach civics in French schools, "to speak seriously about the duties of citizens." He realized that in the new climate of repudiation and hyper-individualism this would be very difficult. To even propose it, he observed, is to look like one who comes from a lost and distant world. In a sense that is the perfect description of Aron in the last two decades of his life. This noble liberal and principled anti-totalitarian brought a more classical wisdom to bear on the great task of preserving and sustaining a truly liberal order. In my view, if alive today he would not be complacent about a society that has rejected the "reality principle" and that confuses rights with radical, even willful, relativism and self-assertion. And he would not be taken in by the apolitical but hopelessly moralistic fanaticism of a center that is acquiescing in the loss or collapse of authoritative institutions throughout the Western world.

## Philippe Bénéton: Beyond Equality by Default

Philippe Bénéton argues persuasively that we have literally theorized ourselves out of good sense and human decency. If we open our eyes and hearts to the experiences at the foundation of natural justice, we will quickly see that "truth is preferable to the lie, courage to cowardice, honesty to dishonesty, love to cruelty." To deny this palpable fact is to reject reality and to succumb to nihilism. Bénéton tellingly adds that this is not a question of choosing the right "values." Rather, it is a question of perceiving the human world before us, since these virtues are built into the very structure of reality. On the political level, Bénéton eschews both a politics of perfection or absolutism, and "the demon of the absence of the Good." The Good is before us but it cannot be fully embodied or instantiated in political or social institutions. But free politics depends upon a morally serious understanding of human dignity, and not an "equality by default" that can say nothing about the virtues and vices of human beings. An authentic liberal society respects pluralism while rejecting what Pope Benedict XVI famously called "the dictatorship of relativism." Between "the demon of the Good" and the

44

"demon of the absence of the Good" lies a politics of prudence worthy of human beings. Such are the metaphysical foundations of moderation, liberty, and human dignity.

As Bénéton remarks, the new moralists laud themselves for their tolerance of difference, compassion for immigrants, opposition to the death penalty, and commitment to saving the planet from ecological destruction. But they show little or no compassion for those on the wrong side of the divide between "progress" and "reaction." It is this dichotomy that has replaced the primordial human distinction between right and wrong, good and evil. Conservatives deserve nothing but opprobrium and marginalization, and victims of Islamist or communist persecution, most especially Christians, are of no concern to them. Some victims are clearly more meritorious than others.

As Aron had already discerned fifty years ago or more, the post-1968 mélange of extreme relativism and extreme moralism cannot sustain a society of free and responsible citizens. The new morality masquerades as a project of emancipation even as it makes its adherents slaves of the passions and of a new, unforgiving intellectual conformism. Without a minimum of self-respect and self-limitation, how can a free society endure? What common projects, what common good, can be sustained on premises that seem to deny the very existence of a society or polity with its own legitimate claims and rules? What is a free people without patriotic attachments that require affection, loyalty, and sacrifice on the part of citizens? As Aron might say, a free society is still a society, and a polity is first and foremost a community of citizens. To think otherwise is to succumb to delusions.

## Chantal Delsol and the Recovery of the Person

Bénéton's striking analyses are complemented by the elegant personalism of the French political philosopher Chantal Delsol. She was a student of Julien Freund, who like Aron challenged moralistic progressive pieties and thought deeply about the nature of the political. If thinkers such as Bénéton and Pierre Manent renew the dialogue between classical political philosophy, Christian wisdom, and conservative liberalism, Delsol is best understood as a personalist deeply informed by the political lessons of the twentieth century. She has made clear to me that she prefers to speak of a "human condition" rather than an unchanging and perhaps excessively rigid notion of human nature. One of the principal lessons of the twentieth century is that the keystone of European culture rests on the dignity of the human person, "an entity possessing a sacred and inalienable value." In her numerous, elegantly written essays and books, Delsol highlights the degradation of man that occurs when we lose sight of a conception of the human being, "an anthropology," that links rights to duties, and personal freedom to moral conscience.

Delsol argues that the experience of totalitarianism in twentieth-century Europe showed that the "rational systems" of modern morality could not account for those scruples (from the Latin *scrupulus*, or pebble), those little pebbles lodged in the human soul "which bother the moral conscience." Scruples cannot be seen but must be felt if we are to avoid personal and political catastrophes of the first order. For Delsol, we do not rationally establish the moral order. Instead, we participate in it. Moral scruples are those obstacles, noted by the poets and discernible in each human soul, to great, ill-advised projects to remake human beings and societies at will. It is a reality unknown to reductive scientism but at the heart of conscience rightly understood. At the same time, Delsol sees a new paganism at work in what is left of the old West. In her most recent book, *La Fin de la chrétienté*, she doesn't endorse it, but advocates forbearance on the part of those who still believe in the old God and the old morality.

For his part, Pierre Manent attempts in an important recent book, *Natural Law and Human Rights*, to renew a conception of natural law rooted in an Aristotelian understanding of reflective choice, a Christian conception of non-arbitrary conscience, and a phenomenological analysis of the motives, from pleasure and utility to the noble and the just, that inform the free will of human beings. Delsol's defense of conscience is less rational, more "personalistic," and clearly derived from the East-Central European experience with totalitarianism in the last half of the twentieth century. Delsol told me she finds many resources for the recovery of a true and humane anthropology from the dissidents and philosophers she came to know in Poland, the Czech Republic, and Hungary. They experienced the evils that flowed from totalitarian ideologies that insisted that some suspect race or class was responsible for the sum total of human evil.

The best French thought, as opposed to the imposters who have claimed that title for at least two generations or more, has renewed an older wisdom that recognizes that human beings are moral, rational, and political animals, responsible persons as opposed to prisoners of biological and sociological determinism or historical necessity, on the one hand, or wholly "autonomous" or self-creating agents, on the other. Liberalism, at its best, always presupposed that most human beings would live in accord with such a balanced and humanizing understanding. This is the "moral capital" that liberalism once presupposed but now actively and aggressively undermines. The new morality, the culture of repudiation, and equality by default (as Philippe Bénéton calls it), all presuppose an empty liberty which can dispose of all ends and purposes outside of pure freedom itself. Such an understanding is compatible with totalitarianism and moral anarchism, but not with political or civilized liberty. To preserve the preconditions of liberty, something more is needed than a voluntarism that no longer recognizes that the non-negotiable distinction between good and evil is a given of our human nature or condition, and not a convention or choice of our own making. On that premise or foundation, everything stands or falls. Such is the wisdom of liberal conservatism.

## Pierre Manent: Beyond Western Self-Contempt

Like Bénéton and Delsol, Manent effortlessly bridges political, philosophical, and theological concerns. He is France's, and perhaps the West's, most astute critic of the de-politicization and de-Christianization of a Western world in the process of losing its sense of animating purpose. As a political thinker, he owes much to Aron's liberal classicism as we have noted. As a critic of radical modernity, he is indebted to Leo Strauss's recovery of classical or Socratic political science. As a convert to Catholicism, he has also been shaped by the Christian classics from St. Augustine and Pascal to Charles Péguy. He played a major role in recovering political liberalism in the France of the 1980s, showing a clear preference for Tocqueville's admirable efforts to ally democratic justice with a more than residual concern for human greatness. In the conclusion of his 1982 *Tocqueville and the Nature of Democracy*—a minor modern classic in my view—he summed up Tocqueville's contribution in a wonderfully lapidary formulation: "To love democracy well, it is necessary to love it moderately." Such is the fundamental insight

47

of liberalism informed by classical and conservative wisdom. This has nothing to do what contemporary integralists clumsily and polemically disparage as "Right Liberalism."

In his wise and provocative 2015 book, *Situation de la France*, translated into English a year later as *Beyond Radical Secularism*, Manent challenges the fundamental conceit of European progressivism for a generation or more: "a life without law in a world without borders." Democracy, too, needs a body, a political form, and that body is the nation that for several centuries or more has framed and informed the exercise of democratic self-government. Manent is convinced that massive Muslim immigration to Europe has been ill-advised, to say the least. But the problem has been exacerbated by the unwillingness of French and European elites to acknowledge "the Christian mark" of the old nations of Europe. Manent speaks precisely: not of a Christian nation or Christian state, for the secular state and religious liberty are indeed precious acquisitions that are essential to Western liberty. But the "Christian mark" of France and Europe is more real and substantial than distant "roots" that one occasionally nods to in rhetorical displays empty of practical significance. It was Christian peoples, Manent suggests, who embarked on the great adventure of self-government, learning to govern themselves *in a certain relation to the Christian proposition*. The European peoples are truly themselves when they do justice to courage and prudence, the great Roman virtues, *and* to humility before the Most High, whose grace informs our exercise of free will and conscience. Such a West, faithful to its deepest purposes, could welcome the Islamic minority on its own terms, not confusing itself with an "empty space," an effectual wasteland without a soul or sense of common purpose.

A nation of a Christian mark can renew the civic common good, preserving fundamental liberties, while humanely navigating the ongoing tensions between liberty and law. Instead, the guardians of political and historical correctness irresponsibly confuse "the community of 'blood and soil' with the political nation and spiritual communion." How, Manent asks, have we succumbed to the sophism that the old nations of Europe somehow stand for "homicidal aversion" to one's neighbors? Such homicidal aversion, culminating in mass murder, occurred only when a new ideological paganism rejected the entire moral and philosophical heritage of liberal and Christian Europe. Nazism, or communism for that matter, is not the effectual truth of Western civilization. To say so is to succumb to a new and terrible ideological lie, and reflects pathological self-contempt, the very *oikophobia* evoked by Roger Scruton.

In a recent conversation with Pierre Manent, I asked him about contemporary European self-hatred. He responded with eloquence and gusto, noting the contemporary European capacity for endless self-deception. In the culture of repudiation, nay of barely concealed self-hatred, European progressives see the victory of European values and inexorable progress "toward a united and fraternal world." To love the old nations and the old religions (Christian and Jewish) is to be "tribal," "indigenous," narrow. As a result, these denizens of Western self-contempt lack the capacity to see what is unfolding before their eyes. Limitless Muslim immigration is transformed into "openness to human diversity," and even a welcome opportunity to flee, once and for all, what is left of the Christian heritage of the West. European progressives freely identify it with oppression, inhuman restraints on individual desire, and crimes against the always ill-defined "Other." One is obliged to uncritically affirm the "Other" while always disparaging one's own.

In this distorted logic, a most tenuous link is established between the old nations (and the old religions) and Nazism, the deadly enemy of an authentically Christian (and liberal) understanding of human dignity. When the accomplishments of Western civilization are truly recognized, when paralyzing self-criticism is balanced with self-respect and with gratitude towards our civilizational patrimony, the new humanitarians can see only indulgence to the crimes of colonialism or Nazism. To refute these charges or allegations, authentic democracy must repudiate its history, and open its borders to all comers. As the old nations and Christianity, the old religion par excellence, lose their legitimacy among European elites, the antipathy to nationalism of the most moderate kind, and to Christianity in an extremely weakened form, grows in ferocity and intensity. These healthy reminders of the permanent necessity to balance tradition and innovation, freedom and self-restraint, liberty and law, must be erased from the consciousness of men. Self-contempt becomes increasingly furious and despotic, hateful of any effort to resist repudiation.

Manent boldly suggests, and it is difficult to challenge his assertion, that the French and European political and intellectual class, in its dominant form, will be satisfied with nothing less than "an empty world without nations or religions." Except, he adds, Islam, whose presence is welcomed by some as a sign that Europeans are truly leaving behind a recognizably Christian world. Such reasoning is surreal, but it has taken hold of many minds and souls in the contemporary West. It has all the zeal of a pernicious "secular religion."

In a series of learned yet accessible writings in political philosophy, Manent has traced the early modern ambition to build a "neutral and agnostic state" freed from religious disputation and the threat of religious wars. But the Western nation-state was never merely the epiphenomenal expression of these liberal philosophical abstractions. For many centuries, liberal societies honored inherited moral judgments and conceded that the citizens of the emerging secular state were for the most part Christians who took Christian morality seriously. The liberal state learned to coexist with Christianity, in its different forms, and was rescued from utopian abstractions by its coexistence with national forms that preceded secular liberalism in its most aggressive forms. (For example, St. Louis and St. Joan of Arc have something to do with the self-definition and self-understanding of the French nation.) Christianity and the political nation taught the citizens of the new liberal democratic dispensation that freedom and human dignity depended upon a thoughtful and principled "compromise between liberty and law."

As Manent writes in his recent book, *Natural Law and Human Rights*, human rights once gave vitality and energy to liberal societies. But under conditions of radical modernity, the new catechism of the rights of man, groundless and endless in extension, undermines political debate and deliberations (rights claims, no matter how spurious, trump all other considerations). And the "rules" that constitute authoritative institutions—the liberal university, the army, the nation itself—are subverted when one can join an institution, or immigrate to a nation, without accepting the specific rules or laws that define free and self-governing social bodies. When the unreflective will of the individual forces authoritative institutions to lose any capacity for command or self-definition, the great art of association heralded by Tocqueville begins to lose its meaning. At that precise moment, democracy has turned against itself, hollowing out the institutions whose health and well-being were once its *raison d'être*. In my judgment, Manent has theorized the human and political meaning of liberty without law with rare accuracy, philosophic acumen, and civic seriousness.

## Renewing the Conservative Underpinnings of the Liberal Order

How does one respond to this new situation, where liberalism has become oppressively illiberal, appropriated by the forces of the new morality and the culture of repudiation? Pierre Manent suggests a self-conscious effort to renew the old conservative underpinnings of the liberal order. In his view, the commanding heights of the social order will continue to be dominated by the forces of moral and civic subversion for some time to come. But "experience and good sense are nonetheless on the side of the conservatives, or the conservative liberals." Even if a statesman of Gaullist temperament arose to make good use of a healthy, conservative-minded populism, the courts and other instruments of the new antinomianism would block all roads forward. Another way must be found.

Chantal Delsol, for her part, has argued that the party of good sense must affirm the limits that accompany a decent and humane liberty, and eschew a merely defensive populism. But some kind of populism seems inescapable in the midst of Europe's sustained civilizational crisis. As Manent puts it, it is imperative that a substantial part of society remains committed to "a minimum of good sense," to the lessons of common sense and practical experience at the heart of civilized liberty. That portion of society, bigger than a remnant but too small and fragile to form a firm moral and civic consensus, can slowly but surely begin to renew the effort of political action at the service of the practical goods that give liberty its nobility and luster. Philippe Bénéton also speaks about the need to refurbish a modern conservatism worthy of the name. Liberal conservatives, or conservative liberals (the difference between the two will not preoccupy us here), reject both unconditional traditionalism and radical constructivism. They honor the truth underlying modern equality but refuse to identify it with indeterminate or groundless freedom which is, always and everywhere, an invitation to nihilism. Liberal conservatives reject the "sovereignty of the individual" since the "unregulated will," as Bertrand de Jouvenel called it, can never give rise to a common good. The "regulated will" is the moral stance

51

appropriate to a regime of liberty and to a truthful understanding of human freedom and responsibility.

The French polymath, historian of ideas, and erudite student of philosophy and religion, Rémi Brague, has also suggested a middle path between hidebound traditionalism and the Promethean project to remake men and societies at a stroke. Nonetheless, he acknowledges a truth in the piety towards the past put forward by traditionalists. All efforts to remake human beings on the model of a *tabula rasa* lead to disaster: What remains of socialist society, he asks? His answer stings in its directness and truthfulness: "There remains only the desert, and charnel-houses." Brague's suggested alternative is both sober and moderate: rejecting a nihilistic contempt for the past, promoting moderate reforms rather than wholesale cultural and political transformation, and recognizing that true democracy honors tradition since it gives "the most obscure of all classes, our ancestors," a living say in the great human adventure, as Chesterton argued in Chapter 4 of his 1908 classic *Orthodoxy*. There, Chesterton memorably called tradition "the democracy of the dead," and he was no hidebound traditionalist or reactionary.

In a delightful book, *Moderately Modern*, translated into English several years ago, Brague reminds us that the practical goods that are abundantly evident in modern life—political liberty, moral equality, prosperity, and scientific progress—should not be confused with the more intellectually radical "Modern Project" that promotes liberty without law and that cannot give an effective answer to the question of why the human adventure ought to continue. As with all of my French interlocutors highlighted in this essay, Brague believes that liberal practice was, for a very long time at least, decisively superior to *modern theory*. In response to this quandary, Brague believes that we need to renew our confidence in the Providence of God, the ultimate ground for human hope since an affirmation of God's Providential care is, at the same time, a vote of confidence in human dignity rooted in free will, conscience, and the grace of God. Quoting André Malraux in *The Kingdom of Man*, also recently available in English, Brague points out that the various modern forms of "moderate nihilism" have played themselves out. Both Pierre Manent and Rémi Brague argue that only renewed confidence in the Primacy of the Good (something than can take more secular and more expressly theological forms) can point us towards a renewal of a hope that owes nothing to the modern fiction of inexorable "Progress." Hope begins by rejecting the ultimate chimera that is a this-worldly utopia, whether in the form of totalitarian despotism or a liberty that rejects the "moral law" that is always inherent in the responsible exercise of human freedom. With this simultaneous rejection and affirmation, Roger Scruton is in full agreement with that humane current of French thought (highlighted in this chapter) that rejects "May 1968" and all its works. For this reason, among others, conservative-minded Frenchmen now pay more and more attention to Scruton's books which have begun to appear in French translation in recent years.

## Sources and Suggested Readings

I have drawn on Roger Scruton's discussion of the best and worst currents of French political and philosophical thought in *Conversations with Roger Scruton*, Roger Scruton and Mark Dooley (London: Bloomsbury, 2016), especially pp. 104–07. On the theme of the worst currents of contemporary political and philosophical thought, especially the representatives of the Parisian "nonsense machine," there is no better resource to draw upon than Roger Scruton's *Fools, Frauds and Firebrands: Thinkers of the New Left* which was published by Bloomsbury Continuum in 2015 (and in paperback in 2019).

Raymond Aron's *La révolution introuvable* (Paris: Calmann-Levy, 2018) did for the "events" of May 1968 what Tocqueville did for the revolution of 1848, namely, to subject it to the withering analysis this half-revolution so richly deserved. Aron's *Liberté et égalité: Cours au Collège de France*, edited and introduced by Pierre Manent, is the best short guide to Aron's mature conservative liberalism.

For astute sociological reflections on democracy and the nation, and the "corruption" (the term is Montesquieu's) of democracy inherent in late modernity, see Dominique Schnapper, *Community of Citizens* (New Brunswick, NJ: Transaction Publishers, 1998) and Schnapper, *The Democratic Spirit of Law*, with a Preface by Mark Lilla (New Brunswick, NJ: Transaction Publishers, 2016).

This chapter draws on years of discussion with, and reflection on, the work of the French philosophers under consideration. I am also grateful to Giulio de Ligio, Philippe Bénéton, Chantal Delsol, Pierre Manent, and Rémi Brague for thoughtfully addressing a series of questions that I posed to them in the fall of 2019.

Philippe Bénéton's critique of "equality by default" and the "new morality" is most fully and effectively presented in Bénéton, *Le déréglement moral de l'occident* (Paris: Editions du Cerf, 2017). An earlier and more concise version of this work appeared in English as Bénéton, *Equality by Default: An Essay on Modernity as Confinement*, translated by Ralph C. Hancock (Wilmington, DE: ISI Books, 2004).

I have learned from all of Chantal Delsol's writings. But I am particularly indebted to Delsol, *The Unlearned Lessons of the Twentieth Century: An Essay on Late Modernity*, translated by Robin Dick (Wilmington, DE: ISI Books, 2006), especially pp. 1, 5, 7, 54, and 178–82.

Pierre Manent's most lucid and accessible critiques of "liberty without law and a world without borders" can be found in Manent, *Beyond Radical Secularism: How France and the Christian West Should Respond to the Islamic Challenge*, translated by Ralph C. Hancock (South Bend, IN: St. Augustine's Press, 2016) and Manent, *Natural Law and Human Rights: Toward a Recovery of Practical Reason*, translated by Ralph C. Hancock (South Bend, IN: University of Notre Dame Press, 2020). I have written "Forewords" to both of these volumes.

For this essay, I am indebted to Rémi Brague, *Moderately Modern*, translated by Paul Seaton (South Bend, IN: St. Augustine's Press, 2019).

For a rather uncritical account of Eric Zémmour's speech to the Convention of the Right in Paris in the fall of 2019, see Rod Dreher, "Eric Zémmour's Blockbuster Speech," at *The American Conservative*, on-line, October 3, 2019. The failure of Zémmour's 2022 candidacy for the French presidency perhaps reveals the limits of his approach and appeal.

# Chapter 4

## DEFENDING THE WEST IN ALL ITS AMPLITUDE: THE LIBERAL CONSERVATIVE VISION OF ROGER SCRUTON

### Becoming a Conservative

As we have discussed in earlier chapters, Roger Scruton dates his turn to conservatism to May 1968, when as a young teacher in France he witnessed a violent and lawless assault on bourgeois civilization that was championed by wild-eyed intellectuals who dreamed of a "radical freedom" allegedly made possible by the rejection of the customs, culture, and institutions of liberal and Christian civilization. Like the conservative-minded liberal Raymond Aron, the most eloquent and forceful critic of the anarcho-Marxism of the time and the scourge of May 1968, the liberal conservative that Roger Scruton now became sided with General de Gaulle and the defense of property, law, and the full range of authoritative institutions that allowed for ordered freedom. Scruton came to appreciate the "real but relative freedom" of the liberal order and the illusory character of the "absolute freedom" dreamed up by "la pensée de soixante-huit"—a freedom somehow compatible with unqualified admiration for totalitarian despotism in Castro's Cuba and Mao's China. Still a young man, Scruton refused the allure of paradoxical and pseudoscientific ideologies that proclaimed with limitless dogmatism that science, law, order, and truth "are merely masks for bourgeois domination." Confronted by "new theories" that attacked the West as a unique instantiation of exploitation and repression, Scruton became—and remains—a partisan of Western civilization. But his conservatism did not develop out of thin air. His working-class father was the kind of patriot described by George Orwell in *The Lion and the Unicorn*: he loved his country instinctively and had no time of day for proletarian revolution. His father was attached to the country-side and the history and architecture of High Wycombe where he lived. He was, in Robert Conquest's formulation, a conservative about all those things he knew deeply. Even before the transformative effects of his sojourn in Paris in the spring and summer of 1968, Roger Scruton appreciated high culture, the need for considered judgment in philosophy, art, music, and architecture, and the need "to conserve the great tradition of the masters." Like his father, he was "right-wing" about the things he knew and cared about. Of course, in the years after 1968, the things Scruton knew and cared about would expand to make room for an impressive command of politics, art, aesthetics, architecture, music, and of course, philosophy. Scruton is one of the few serious political thinkers of our time. However, he is so much more than a mere "political theorist," to use the rather flat locution of the academy. He is at once a philosopher of the first rank and an artful practitioner of humane letters.

Scruton has laid out his liberal conservative vision in a series of books from *The Meaning of Conservatism* (1979) to *How To Be a Conservative* (2014). He was no foe of the renewed defense of civil society (and critique of collectivism) put forward by Prime Minister Margaret Thatcher in the years between 1979 and 1990. But he wanted to expand the horizons of conservatism, to remind his fellow conservatives that "freedom" cannot be the all-encompassing answer to what conservatives believe in. In *How to be a Conservative* he quotes Matthew Arnold's wonderfully arresting remark that "freedom is a very good horse to ride, but to ride *somewhere*." Conservatism, properly understood, has something to say about the civilized ends and purposes of human freedom. It does not rest content with groundless freedom as the goal of a life worthy of human beings. Nor was Scruton content with the individualist rhetoric that distorted the otherwise salutary goals of Thatcher and Thatcherism. There really is a "society" and the defense of the "little platoons" and subsidiary institutions between the state and the individual is one of the principal tasks of conservatism in the modern world. To her great credit, Thatcher was also a patriot and a partisan of national loyalty. She did not succumb to the "*oikophobia*"—the hatred of home and country—beloved by so many intellectuals. Indeed, one of Roger Scruton's great achievements has been to theorize national loyalty and patriotic attachment in a way that shows that our moral and political choices are in no way exhausted by a false and thankless choice between xenophobia and *oikophobia.*

## Resistance to Totalitarianism

Antitotalitarianism is a fundamental feature of Scruton's liberal conservative vision. He worked closely with unofficial networks (the intellectual underground) in Poland, Hungary, and Czechoslovakia (especially the latter), and he came to know the depredations of "really existing socialism" from the inside. This was a world where socialism was imposed by force and ritualistically incanted lies. Scruton admired Jan Patočka, Václav Havel, Václav Benda, and other great dissident thinkers and activists, and he bore witness to their efforts to expose the ideological Lie and to recover the memory of great and ancient peoples and nations. He translated one of Havel's greatest essays "Politics and Conscience" from the original Czech into English, and he played an important role in educating Havel and others about the problematic intentions of Western "peace movements," blind as they were to the nature of totalitarian regimes at home and abroad. Havel's 1985 essay "Anatomy of a Reticence," his brilliant dissection of the moral ambiguities of Western peace movements, owes much to his dialogue with Benda and Scruton on this matter.

Confronting underground intellectuals in Central Europe, Scruton saw a harried and harassed group of men and women with whom he "felt an immediate affinity." Forbidden to publish, fired from their jobs, and largely working as stokers in factories, apartment buildings, and industrial complexes, they pursued the truth (never in scare quotes as with our postmodernist intellectuals) and bore witness to the evils of totalitarianism. Their underground writings were an exercise in what Plato called *anamnesis*: "the bringing to consciousness of forgotten things." They wished to recover the experiences of the soul in all their amplitude and to affirm the full continuities of national and European life. Patočka's *Plato and Europe*, a book that reached the West long before it was published in a free Czechoslovakia after 1989, is a paradigmatic example of this effort to recover "the care of the soul" at the heart of the West, a task that was under brutal and systematic assault from politicized atheism and totalitarian collectivism. Scruton bore witness to the "dissidents" and made their plight—and intellectual and moral witness—known to the Western world. For that, he has been justly honored by the Czech government. His scintillating account of that now forgotten world of tyranny and dissent is told with sweet sadness and literary grace in his 2014 novel *Notes from Underground*. This is a book that rewards close reading and reflection and makes the experience of "the soul of man under socialism" available to all. Only Roger Scruton could have told this story. He has done it extraordinarily well. It has been published in Czech to some critical acclaim. We will explore this masterwork at length in a subsequent chapter.

## A Good European and a Euroskeptic

Scruton is the model of what Nietzsche called the "good European." Always attentive to our present circumstances, he brings the full riches of the Western intellectual tradition to bear on the pathologies that confront our civilization. He sees the spark of the transcendent in the mundane world, the intimations of the sacred in a world reduced to matter in motion. As someone who recognizes the dignity and grandeur of Kant's philosophical project, he doesn't conflate the noumenal and phenomenal realms. As importantly, he does not deny their mysterious and humanizing points of contact. Scruton has a capacious idea of Europe, one with a place for a Christianity with, what Solzhenitsyn called at Harvard, "its rich reserves of mercy and sacrifice," and the true democracy and accountability made possible by self-governing nation-states. For Scruton, the failed European constitution of 2005 revealed the absurdity of defining the European idea in abstraction from the Christian religion, and the "democratic deficit" that is coextensive with the European project, particularly in its post-Maastricht form. European elites seem determined to act as if the European adventure began in 1968. To be a "good European" today, to avoid the twin extremes of xenophobia and *oikophobia*, it is necessary to resist a Europe-Behemoth that erodes the wellsprings of civilized order and weakens the nation-state, the only viable home of democratic accountability in the modern world. Here Roger Scruton and Pierre Manent are in the fullest agreement.

As we have suggested, Roger Scruton's political philosophizing is marked by a judicious melding of conservatism and liberalism. Like his great predecessor (and inspiration) Burke, he defends a regime of liberty that is conscious of its debts to a civilization that is not reducible to contract and consent alone. He defends the secular character of the modern state in a decisive manner. But he also knows that secularism undermines itself when it actively repudiates the Christian inheritance of the West. He appreciates that the free and responsible individual is unthinkable without a political community that grounds the reciprocal obligations of free men and women. Standing athwart the culture of repudiation beloved by the Left and critical of the libertarian abstractions that increasingly deform conservatism, Scruton articulates a liberal conservatism that balances commitment to territorial democracy, the self-governing nation-state, and support for those mediating institutions between the state and the individual that give life to active citizenship.

## The Good Side of Government

Scruton's liberal conservatism, equally distant from leftist antinomianism and libertarian idolatry of the self-subsisting individual, is beautifully expressed in an essay on "Governing Rightly" that appears in his 2016 collection of essays, *Confessions of a Heretic*. This graceful essay is a friendly but forceful warning to conservatives not to despise government and politics, not to succumb to the Rousseau-inspired illusion that "men are born free" and will only achieve their full capacities as authentic individuals if government and other authoritative institutions get out of the way. Like much of the cultural Left, many on the Right have mistakenly come to identify politics with power and domination. Having courageously resisted the destructive cultural project of the Left in the 1960s, the political and intellectual Right are presently in danger of capitulating to one of its most destructive philosophical presuppositions. Today, the old conservative insight that the exercise of true authority is diametrically opposed to arbitrariness and authoritarianism, that order is the other side of freedom, is in danger of being forgotten by *soi-disant* conservatives. Scruton sets out to recover an older and richer conception of liberty that owes much to conservatism properly understood.

Scruton stands with American conservatives in rejecting a "European model" of the relation of the individual and the state. The European state has come to embody "state-imposed orthodoxies" that have little respect for common morality or "the old and settled customs" of a millennial-old civilization. As with the American Left, abortion on demand and "same-sex marriage" are simply taken for granted as fundamental human rights, and the moral consensus of the ages is disregarded. As a result, religious liberty is under threat and a ubiquitous regime of political correctness shows little tolerance for dissent. Not pulling his punches, Scruton refers to a "hysteria of repudiation" that rages among European intellectual and political elites. Contemporary liberals increasingly show contempt for the salutary conservative foundations of the democratic order. Even as the moral foundations of democracy are being systematically and deliberately eroded, small businesses and the ordinary enterprises of hardworking citizens are under assault from a bureaucratic state that is suspicious of individual initiatives as such. Scruton is quick to point out that the European model leads to "emasculated societies" and that American conservatives are right to be deeply suspicious of such a "European" future.

The problem, Scruton argues, is that many American Conservatives identify the European model with government as such and have little to say about the "good side" of government. They have lost sight of the fact that government is natural to the human condition and reflects "extended loyalties" that connect the living to the dead as well as to the yet to be born (in Burke's admirably capacious understanding of the true social contract that unites civilized human beings and that keeps at bay the tyranny of the living). Government is the indispensable vehicle for mutual commitment and public spirit among human beings who are accountable to each other. Even our rights are unthinkable without a government to enforce them, including the ability to enforce them against itself. Order, legitimate authority, is not coextensive with power and domination as Foucault on the Left and some libertarian ideologues on the Right insist. And while the nation-state, or territorial democracy, provides the indispensable framework of rule-of-law societies, government is already present in the "little platoons" praised by Burke in his *Reflections on the Revolution in France* and in the free associations of citizens and neighbors highlighted by Alexis de Tocqueville in *Democracy in America*. (Like Tocqueville, Scruton is a partisan of the nation and a localist at the same time.) Ayn Rand's fevered narratives of heroic entrepreneurs "removing the shackles of government" and returning to a state of nature where they will flourish as human gods is "the opposite of the truth." Her books describe a cold and less than human world without mutual accountability and thus ordered or civilized freedom.

We human beings are not free—or truly human—in a "state of nature." True individuality cannot flourish outside a legal and moral framework that unites free consent with the full range of our mutual obligations to each other (the affinities with Pierre Manent here are quite striking). The liberal conservative adamantly refuses to conflate legitimate authority with authoritarianism or "domination." Human beings are not accountable in a state of nature—they are laws unto themselves—and are wholly lacking in self-knowledge. They are not yet aware that human beings, however suspicious of government, "have yet deeper need for it." "Government is wrapped into the very fibres of our social being." Authentic individuality—as opposed to atomistic individualism—needs a social and political context that it forgets at its own peril. In social and political life we are obliged to give an account of ourselves, even as government is obliged to give an account of its doings to citizens. The accountability characteristic of rule-of-law societies and self-governing nations prevents government from becoming the engine of exploitation that ideologues on the Left and the Right always assume that it is.

With the Arab Spring of 2011, we saw the fall of Middle Eastern governments bereft of public spirit and a developed sense of accountability. These authoritarian regimes were in most cases replaced by a new set of "bullies and fanatics" who were inspired by an even less sufficient sense of the mutual accountability that informs true political life. One version of Kant's "categorical imperative," our duty to treat other rational beings as ends and not means, helps us clarify the "web of rights and duties" that informs a truly free society. People only become free when they take responsibility for their actions. The autonomous individual in the vulgar sense of the term, beholden to nothing but his idiosyncratic whims and wishes, is the very opposite of a morally responsible citizen in a free society. For Scruton, sovereign individuals are "also obedient subjects." They are accountable to others and must defer to the requirements of the moral law. This is very close to what Pierre Manent calls "liberty under law," law capaciously understood.

In Scruton's lapidary formulation, "government and freedom have a single source, which is the human disposition to hold each other to account for what we do." America is the "land of the free" not because it is or has ever been free of government but because it has the kind of government that allows for true human accountability. Even "the associative habits" praised by Tocqueville are not a substitute for government. Citizens acting together without commands from the central authorities point to a form of self-government that codifies and amplifies the responsibilities of citizens to each other. Authentic conservative thought accordingly entails a defense of liberty and a defense of government as its indispensable handmaiden. In Scruton's view, conservatives should criticize a view of government that confiscates freedom and undermines the responsibilities and accountability of self-governing citizens. At the same time, they are obliged to put forward a humanizing political alternative. Today, "conservatism should be a *defense* of government, against its abuse by liberals."

## A Conservative Welfare State

That "does not mean that conservatives are wedded to some libertarian conception of the minimal state." The welfare state has spawned pathologies that conservatives ought to vigorously oppose. A culture of dependency erodes self-government and personal responsibility. Thus, efforts must be made to balance the state's obligation to care for the most vulnerable among us (especially those who can't take care of themselves) with the accountability that must be asked even of the poorest of the poor (contra left-wing social science and advocacy, all of us—rich and poor—are accountable as citizens and moral agents). But the welfare state should not be condemned in principle. This is to succumb to an individualism that rejects the mutual accountability at the heart of civil society. In England, the nation that Scruton knows best, the needy and indigent fought for Britain and civilized liberty in two world wars. The political community owes something to its neediest citizens and to those who gave of themselves in defense of their country. This is the meaning of the social contract, or true reciprocity, in the best and highest sense of those terms. But this qualified conservative defense of the welfare state should not be confused with the kind of redistributionist state outlined by John Rawls that punishes success and undermines personal responsibility in the name of an abstract vision of "fairness." This is a "theory of justice" that is fundamentally unjust. And Scruton's position has nothing to do with perpetuating a "culture of dependency" that breaks up families and hurts the poorest of the poor. Scruton's liberal conservatism supports a humane economy and a modest but effective welfare state. Public spirit in this capacious vision never aims to starve private initiative (or the public sector for the matter), but rather to link public spirit to the associative habits of free and responsible citizens. It never argues for freedom *from* government but for "another and better form of government" worthy of morally serious human beings who unite public spirit and private initiative in the judicious mix appropriate to a modern regime of liberty. We can properly call this vision of public philosophy "liberal conservatism."

## Conserving the Nation and the National Patrimony

As we have already noted, Roger Scruton is an admirer of Margaret Thatcher, yet he can't be said to be a Thatcherite, at least in any narrow sense of the term. Better than almost anyone else, he has discerned the moral core of her greatness. Her most important speeches as well as her most enduring policies "stemmed from a consciousness of national loyalty," a consciousness very dear to Scruton himself. She and her advisors too often used the cold and desiccated language of economic rationality: "market solutions," "consumer sovereignty," and the rest. However, she was first and foremost a patriot who believed in England and its institutions "and saw them as the embodiment of social affections nurtured and stored over centuries." "The pity was that she had no philosophy" with which to articulate her deepest convictions and affirmations. But far from being a libertarian ideologue, "family, civil association, the Christian religion and the common law were all integrated into her ideal of freedom under law." It would not be going too far to suggest that Roger Scruton's liberal conservatism best accounts for what is true and enduring in Mrs. Thatcher's vision. We will have more to say about this in another chapter.

Scruton wants to conserve the nation as the vehicle of self-government and political civilization and the right kind of government as an essential part of the economy of human freedom. Conservatives conserve civilization. They conserve the government of free men and women. As such, they ought to be committed to conserving nature. Scruton does not see the environment as a "left-wing cause at all." Environmentalism, properly understood, aims to safeguard resources. It is not about "liberation" or enforced equality. Rather, it is about conservation and equilibrium. Socialism, "with its gargantuan, uncorrectable and state-controlled projects" is far more threatening to a balanced ecology than the ethos of free enterprise, as the ecological devastation proffered by Soviet-style economies undeniably show. True ecologists favor decentralization and want to conserve what is best about home, the concrete world where real human beings live. They are suspicious of grand planning with its contempt for local perspectives and initiatives. Scruton's ecological vision in a book like *How to Think Seriously about the Planet* is ultimately Burkean: environmentalism is the "quintessential conservative cause" because it is the "most vivid instance" that we know of a "partnership between the dead, the living, and the unborn, which Burke defended as the conservative archetype." Once again, Scruton enlarges the contemporary conservative vision by freeing it from an economism and present-mindedness that is good neither for society nor the soul. He is an environmentalist or ecologist, rightly understood, and an impressive guide for conservatives in that regard.

## The Political Nation versus Toxic Nationalism

Pierre Manent has long observed that scholars and pundits are preoccupied with the most pathological expressions of nationalism even as they ignore the nation as the "political form" that allows democratic self-government to flourish in the modern world. Manent and Scruton share in common the rare ability to distinguish between humane national loyalty (the love of country and the willingness to defend it) and the nationalist distortion of national loyalty. Manent and Scruton insist that this is "not its normal condition." The partisans of antipolitical cosmopolitanism see the leaving behind of the nation-state as the essential precondition for a "lasting peace." They simply assume that transnational political entities will be peaceful, although there is no real evidence to support this claim. Manent speaks of the misplaced reduction of the political alternatives to "blood and soil" nationalism, to radical forms of rootedness or autochthony, and a rootlessness that denies the necessarily political context of humanity and human belonging. The political nation and the "spiritual communion" that informed it has little, or nothing, to do with "toxic nationalisms" and the "exclusive valorization of one's people and homicidal aversion for people from elsewhere." Only a nihilistic repudiation of the Biblical God and a moral law above the human will could give rise to such murderous and self-destructive nationalism. Manent argues that the nations of the West always tied self-government to the Christian proposition, and free will and conscience to the friendship and Providence of the Most High. The secularism of the modern state for a long time presupposed the Christian character of Western civilization (this theme is explicit in Manent's work and implicit in the full range of Scruton's reflection). The nation could not be the highest locus of human aspiration until the Christian proposition had lost credibility among Western elites. Only then could the nation become an idol.

Scruton, too, believes that it is a terrible mistake to identify the self-governing nation with the most frenzied and tyrannical expressions of nationalism, such as the French nation under Jacobin captivity or the German nation under Hitler. The latter had succumbed to "anger, resentment, and fear" fueled by a murderous denial of the moral law. Scruton pointedly describes the poisoning of the German soul: "All Europe was threatened by the German nation, but only because the German nation was threatened by itself." Like Manent, Scruton believes that national loyalty is not inherently aggressive or belligerent: it does not deny, in principle, the legitimacy of other peoples' national self-affirmation. As Scruton puts it in his important essay "Conserving Nations," "national loyalty involves a love of home and a preparedness to defend it." In contrast, nationalism is a "belligerent ideology, which uses national symbols in order to conscript the people to war." As Chesterton and Scruton have noted, nations can go mad even as lovers can kill, but it would be the height of absurdity to condemn patriotism or love because of the crimes committed in their names. Every friend of "liberty under God" and of self-government rightly understood knows that the "modern horrors" associated with pathological nationalism demands not the evacuation of the nation but a return to a proper understanding of the political and spiritual goods and humanizing limits that properly inform it.

## Territorial Membership versus Creedal and Tribal Identifications

Scruton carefully distinguishes national or territorial forms of membership from tribal and creedal varieties. Citizens are settled in a certain circumscribed territory. They share "language, institutions, customs and a sense of history" and they "regard themselves as equally committed both to the place of residence and to the legal and political processes that governs it." For Scruton, citizens are granted "security and freedom in exchange for consent" (which often is of a tacit character). Members of a religious community, in contrast, are subjects; they *submit* to religious or divine law (Scruton clearly has Islam in mind where religious affirmation is coextensive with submission to a profoundly willful if "Compassionate" God). National loyalty necessarily "marginalizes loyalties of family, tribe, and faith, and places before the citizen's eyes, as the focus of his patriotic feeling, not a person or group but a country." National loyalty is above all territorial loyalty. If members of a tribe see themselves as first and foremost members of a family, if members of "creed communities" see each other above as the faithful, as co-religionists, "members of nations see each other as neighbors." The citizen does not think and act like the member of a tribe, jealously guarding his kin, or the adherent of a creed striking out at infidels and apostates.

## True and False Secularism

In Scruton's view, Christianity separates in principle "the things of God" and "the things of Caesar." It thus prepares the way for the secular jurisdiction of the modern state. He makes much of Christ's words in Matthew 22. Sometimes, Scruton's position reminds one of the French political theorist Marcel Gauchet's paradoxical claim that "Christianity is the religion to leave religion behind," because Christianity prepares the way for the secular state and its own political obsolescence. But Scruton is not that kind of secularist. He believes that national boundaries are "precious" and yet he affirms that the civilization that has made "national boundaries perceivable" is even more precious. That civilization is unthinkable without Christianity. To borrow Pierre Manent's language, it is a civilization that brings together the Roman virtues of prudence and courage with mercy and sacrifice and humble deference to God. As Scruton puts it, confession, forgiveness, and repentance, are quintessential parts of the Western soul and the Christian inheritance. The totalitarian systems of the twentieth century, Communism and National Socialism above all, struck at all the virtues, including the pride of the citizen and the Christian acknowledgment of the indispensability of confession and repentance. The nation is not an end in itself. It is not an idol that is the final locus of human loyalties and aspirations. It is a "concrete universal," as Manent likes to put it, that points beyond itself without ever negating the intrinsic goods—courage, civic friendship, sacrifice, citizenship—associated with humane national loyalty.

The European Union continues to efface the Christian mark of Europe, giving rise to the "dictatorship of relativism" lamented by Pope Benedict XVI in 2005, even as it undermines the integrity of the nation and national loyalty. What is needed is a return to national loyalty rooted in the "Judaeo-Christian heritage of the West." To think that the goods of liberty, national loyalty, and civilization can flourish without that Judaeo-Christian heritage "is to live in cloud cuckoo land," as Scruton has forcefully put it.

In my view, Scruton's tendency to overstate the "secularism" of the "nation of a Christian mark" (Pierre Manent) is rooted in the contrast that he habitually draws between Islam and the Christian West. Manent is more explicit in his writings on the necessary coexistence of the secular state and a more than residually Christian nation. In the end I believe Manent and Scruton are saying something quite similar, as Scruton acknowledges in his sympathetic discussion of Manent at the end of his 2018 book: *Conservatism: An Invitation to the Great Tradition*. Both agree that the territorial nation has never really been at home in the Arab Islamic world. Empire, a universalism rooted in *sharia* law and the *umma* of true believers, is the "political form" that is natural to Islam. A state such as Pakistan may sometimes function as a state, but it rarely succeeds in superseding tribal and creedal loyalties. The same is true even of a country like Egypt, where national loyalty is more established and has sometimes challenged Islamic self-assertion. The Western idea of national government and national loyalty is at odds with Islamic conceptions of religious community and Koranic law. Scruton and Manent argue with some plausibility that "the nation state is an anti-Islamic idea."

## Doing Justice to the Goods of the Soul

Neither Scruton nor Manent identify the self-governing nation with radical secularism, with a *laïcité* hostile to the religious heritage of the West, as many secularists (especially but not only in France) are prone to do. Radical secularists want a civilization that is indifferent to religion, which is strictly neutral toward any conceptions of the Good that make demands on our souls. Such a desiccated understanding does not speak to the human soul and is hardly attractive to those in the non-Western world who mistake Western liberty for moral indifference and a soulless materialist cornucopia. Militant secularism repudiates both philosophy and religion and makes the good life coextensive with indifference to truth. (I am here positing that true philosophy presupposes an order of things that is knowable, in part and in principle, to those who seek the truth.) A civilization worthy of the name must affirm truth and liberty at the same time. The Western state and nation is the furthest thing from a confessional or creedal state. Scruton makes that very clear in his work. But the West cannot remain the West if it becomes completely indifferent to moral goods or the life of the soul. Conjugating truth and liberty, while respecting a regime of political consent (and not consent all the way down), is one of the highest tasks of prudence in the modern world. All of this is implicit in Scruton's work. Still, his political philosophy would be even more persuasive if he distinguished more explicitly and emphatically between the good and bad manifestations of secularism in modern times.

## Defending the West

None of this is to suggest that Roger Scruton in any way fails to do justice to the full range of Roman and Christian virtues. He knows the West needs to be defended, and his understanding of the West is most capacious, indeed. In his understanding the West is an "inheritance" that needs to be cultivated, cherished, and protected. In his writings and his work with the antitotalitarian underground in Czechoslovakia and Poland, he worked to save liberty and the human soul from an ideology that was at once an enemy of man and an enemy of civilization. Few thinkers of our time have a deeper understanding of the mendacity at the core of the totalitarian enterprise. One did not fight Communist totalitarianism simply to defend markets or the superior performance of Western economies. Nor was the antitotalitarian fight a struggle for ever-expanding and sometimes groundless and fictive "human rights," rights that are accompanied by no corresponding sense of responsibility. At their best the great moral witnesses in the age of ideology, such as Akhmatova, Pasternak, Havel, and Solzhenitsyn, bore witness to the redemptive presence of truth and beauty, as well as to the vulnerability of the regime of the Lie "to one word of Truth that shall outweigh the world." They taught that men and societies cannot be remade at a stroke, nor can they be reduced to playthings of the historical process. Hatred and cruelty (of a racial or class character) have no ultimate ontological status, no capacity to speak to the deepest recesses of the human soul. The final word belongs neither to mendacity nor moral destruction.

Our civilization admirably withstood the totalitarian assault. But it now suffers largely from self-inflicted wounds. We are unlikely to succumb to a civilization in arrested development that stands for subjecthood rather than citizenship, religious submission rather than national loyalty and religious freedom, a phony solemnity instead of an ironic appreciation of human sins and limits. Scruton reminds us that the West has always been a self-critical civilization, a civilization that succumbs to ideological dogmatism and religious fanaticism at the cost of its soul. We must defend our way of life and respond to the violence of Islamist radicals "with whatever force is required." Like Pierre Manent, Scruton reminds us that salutary self-criticism has nothing to do with pathological self-loathing. A free, self-critical yet self-confident people must defend its civilized inheritance with vigor and without apology.

At the same time, Scruton appreciates that courage and prudence must be accompanied in the private sphere by the spirit of forgiveness that keeps us from reciprocating the hatred and bile put forward by our enemies and ideological foes. We must combine a spirited defense of liberty with the spirit of love and forgiveness taught by Christ. We must not reduce our civilization to the defense of a formless liberty that sits complacently over a moral abyss. That is the path of perdition. Scruton's prudent liberal conservatism, his judicious melding of truth and liberty, his philosophically minded Christianity, and his deference to what is best in our philosophical and religious traditions, point the way forward. He points a listless civilization toward the wisdom of Plato, Kant, Burke, and the great antitotalitarian wisdom and moral witnesses of the twentieth century. In his writings one finds ample material for the renewal of political civilization.

## Sources and Suggested Readings

This chapter draws on many years of sustained reading and critical reflection on Roger Scruton's work. The account of Scruton's movement to his distinctive kind of intellectual and political conservatism draws on "My Journey," the opening chapter of his *How To Be A Conservative* (London: Bloomsbury, 2014), 1–17, especially 3–10. The account of Scruton's engagement with antitotalitarian thought draws on the same text, pages 10–12, and on some beautiful passages in "Faking It" in Scruton's *Confessions of a Heretic* (London: Notting Hill, 2016), 1, 16–17. The reader will also want to consult the discussions on this matter in *Conversations with Roger Scruton*, by Mark Dooley and Roger Scruton (London: Bloomsbury, 2016). *Notes From Underground: A Novel* (New York: Beauford Books, 2014) brilliantly brings the world of Czech dissent to light and reminds us of the permanent lessons to be learned from the totalitarian episode.

My discussions of Scruton's view of the European project and his articulation and defense of the nation and national loyalty draws heavily on "Conserving Nations" in *A Political Philosophy: Arguments for Conservatism* (London: Bloomsbury, 2006), 1–32, and on "Defending the West" in *Confessions of a Heretic*, 172–94. The latter essay also contains helpful discussions of Islam, Christianity, and secularism. See pages 178–79 of "Defending the West" for a discussion of the incompatibility between Islam and national loyalty and pages 181–82 for a discussion of the dialectical relationship between Christianity and modern secularism. My discussion of Scruton's defense of good government against the pathologies of decayed liberalism draws extensively from "Governing Rightly" in *Confessions of a Heretic*, 34–49. For a succinct and eloquent discussion of conservatism and ecology, see "Conserving Nature" in *Confessions of a Heretic*, especially, page 152. For Scruton's reflections on Thatcher and Thatcherism, see *How To Be A Conservative*, 7–10.

For Scruton's most beautiful articulation of the place of confession, forgiveness, and repentance in a Western civilization profoundly marked by Christianity see *How To Be A Conservative*, 15–17. For Pierre Manent's penetrating critique of radical secularism and his defense of the necessary collaboration of courage and prudence with the Christian virtues see sections 12 and 13 of Manent, *Beyond Radical Secularism: How France and the Christian West Should Respond to the Islamic Challenge* (South Bend, IN: St. Augustine's Press, 2016). Section 20 of the same work beautifully differentiates the "nation of a Christian mark" from the anti-Christian and "toxic" nationalisms that succumbed to "homicidal aversion" toward their neighbors.

## Chapter 5
## "IN THE TRUTH OF OUR POLITICAL NATURE": PIERRE MANENT'S DEFENSE OF POLITICAL REASON IN *A WORLD BEYOND POLITICS?*

[A] political regime is always partial, and always repressive in some measure, but it is a certain way of holding together the diverse aspects of human life. Politics allows the diverse experiences to communicate with one another, obliges them to communicate according to the form and the regime. That is why politics is the great mediation or the mediation of mediations. It prevents any experience from claiming absolute validity; it prevents any experience from saturating the social arena and the individual consciousness; it requires any experience to coexist and to communicate with the other experiences. In this way, politics is the guardian of the wealth and complexity of human life. (*A World beyond Politics?*, 201–02 )

The political philosopher Pierre Manent describes his most political book, *Cours familier de philosophie politique*, as a "*tableau raisonné du monde actuel*"—"an analytic overview of the contemporary world" (see the *avant-propos* to the book).[1] The book, which came out in English in 2004 as *A World beyond Politics?: A Defense of the Nation-State*,[2] is a reworking of twenty-two lectures originally delivered at the Institute of Political Studies (*Sciences Po*) in Paris on the "Great Stakes" of modern politics. The gracefully crafted lectures provide nothing less than a comprehensive analysis of

---

1 Pierre Manent, *Cours familier de philosophie politique* (Paris: Fayard, 2001). The title (*A Familiar Course of Political Philosophy*) alludes to a work by the nineteenth-century French writer Lamartine.

2 Manent, *A World beyond Politics? A Defense of the Nation-State*, translated by Marc LePain (Princeton, NJ: Princeton University Press, 2006).

the political condition of modern man. In them, Manent treats the full range of political phenomena: the dynamics of liberal society, debates about equality, the place of religion in officially secular societies, Europe and future of the nation, the wars of the twentieth century, political economy, the nature of democratic individualism, the family and feminism, and the question of totalitarianism. There is, however, nothing superficial or summary about the discussions. The book displays an unforced mastery of the theory and practice of politics, commenting with equal penetration on the texts of Aristotle or the limits of "humanitarian intervention" in Kosovo in the late 1990s.

One of the great charms of the book, as Paul Thibaud has suggested, is Manent's masterly use of the "art of citation."[3] His guides to the study of politics include an impressive range of philosophers, social theorists, and historians—the most cited authors in the text are Rousseau, Marx, Tocqueville, Raymond Aron, and Claude Lefort. We will have more to say about the sources and citations. As a result, the book is the furthest thing from doctrinaire: Manent shows an admirable willingness to learn from all the parties. Those diverse authors are Manent's interlocutors, and in every case, interpretation is linked to the common task of illuminating the dilemmas of democratic modernity. But along the way the book provides an invaluable introduction to political philosophy, even as it keeps its focus steadily on the political world that political philosophy sets out to illuminate.

All of Pierre Manent's writings are a reflection on modern humanity's "liberal destiny." It is our fate to live in a world framed and transformed by the presuppositions of modern liberty. Modern liberty posits a new human world built on the foundation of individual consent, a world of free and equal individuals who affirm their collective sovereignty and individual rights. In important respects, this new world emancipates human beings from old constraints and injustices, even from the idea of an order of command, or so is its pretension. But at the same time it separates human beings, undermining institutions and attachments that gave stability and meaning to human life. In Manent's view, advanced liberal societies increasingly resemble a civilized version of the "state of nature"

---

3   See Paul Thibaud's fine review of *Cours familier* in *L'Express*, 17 janvier 2002, p. 17.

of free and equal individuals posited by the early modern political philosophers such as Thomas Hobbes and John Locke. The theoretical doctrines of revolutionary philosophers have to a remarkable extent become the lived reality of our age. All the old ties—family, religion, and nation—once deemed natural are increasingly attenuated and eroded. They are seen as restraints on freedom rather than its essential preconditions. They lack ultimate legitimacy in a world whose twin lodestars are the rights of the individual and the categorical imperative of sympathetic identification with suffering "humanity." But Manent's analysis is in no way reactionary. Like Roger Scruton's, it provides a conservative correction to some of liberalism's illusions. He places no hopes in a golden age to which it is possible or desirable to return. He acknowledges the intrinsic strengths of the modern dispensation, as well as its significant limitations. Representative government, commercial exchange, and an enhanced sense of fellow feeling create a human order that has been remarkably durable and in many ways choice-worthy. The nineteenth-century French "retrogrades," such as Joseph de Maistre and Louis de Bonald, were wrong to believe that a liberal society could not endure as a viable human association.

But, as Manent points out, the Achilles' heel of the modern order is its failure to appreciate its dependence on moral contents that predate the formation of the liberal state and society. Religion is undoubtedly one such inheritance that gives solidity and content to the dizzyingly formal abstraction of individual consent. And the nation-state is the indispensable political framework in which modern freedom first unfolded. If the nation-state is presently moribund, then Europeans must revivify it or create a new political form to take its place. But Manent insists that the logic of modern freedom is essentially antipolitical or individualistic. Liberalism strives to create a world without political forms or mediations. The antiliberal German political thinker Carl Schmitt famously claimed that there is no such thing as liberal politics, only a liberal critique of politics. Without simply following the German jurist, Manent sees truth in that characterization, as would Alexis de Tocqueville. Following Tocqueville, Manent believes that self-government belongs to the "art" of democracy. If Schmitt condemned liberalism *tout court* and succumbed to the totalitarian temptation out of antiliberal ire, Manent's work seeks to renew the art that is indispensable for a healthy liberal order. Manent does not deny that modern man has a fuller appreciation of the common humanity of human beings than was affirmed or felt by his predecessors. Modern men and women have assuredly experienced moral progress of a sort (as well as unprecedented evils, such as totalitarianism). But as Manent argues in the closing lines of *A World beyond Politics?*, "the promise of moral progress contained in contemporary humanitarian sensibility will remain sterile if we do not know how to delineate the political framework in which it will be able to produce real and lasting effects" (*WBP*, 206). Contemporary Europeans are deluded if they think that they have arrived at the end of history, that they can live in some perfected state of civilization without the mediating presence of politics.

*A World beyond Politics?* builds on Manent's previous writings, and points toward later ones, but stands apart in several important respects. The analysis of modernity is somewhat less abstract and textually focused, and its authorial perspective is more obviously political or civic than some of his earlier writings. The book self-consciously aims to provide a "map" of the contemporary world for the morally serious citizen and statesman. Like Manent's previous writings, it aspires to understand both "the text and the world."[4] But Manent's previous writings took their bearings principally from an analysis of the texts of the Western political and philosophical traditions (although all of Manent's writings display a rich historical sense that is lacking in much contemporary political theory). There is a reason for this. For Manent, a serious engagement with the history of political philosophy is indispensable for self-knowledge, since the liberal world was shaped by the modern philosophical solution to Europe's "theological-political problem." A range of liberal or protoliberal thinkers, from Machiavelli to Hobbes and Locke, believed that it was necessary to conceive a politics closed to the Good to prevent either priestly despotism or socially destructive religious disputations (think, the "wars of religion"). Liberal societies largely took their bearings from this new understanding. The separation of religion and politics, and more fundamentally of power and opinion, is the first of the separations that would come to define the modern political

---

4   See Manent's essay "Toward the Work and Toward the World: Claude Lefort's *Machiavelli*" in Manent, *Modern Liberty and Its Discontents*, edited and translated by Daniel J. Mahoney and Paul Seaton, with an introduction by Daniel J. Mahoney (Lanham, MD: Rowman and Littlefield, 1998), 47–63.

world (*WBP*, 10–20). The separation of religion and politics and power and opinion is the crucial precondition for refounding the political world around the idea of human rights. No specific idea about the human good was to be authoritatively, that is politically, established. Such views were relegated to the private realm of civil society. In chapter 2 of *A World beyond Politics?*, entitled "The Theological-Political Vector," Manent extends the rich analysis of religion and liberalism that he originally sketched in *An Intellectual History of Liberalism*.[5] Drawing on the writings of the contemporary French philosopher Marcel Gauchet, he powerfully highlights the ways in which modern democracy has transformed religion. Religion has increasingly become an expression of one's identity rather than an authoritative guide to the nature of things and the truth about God and man (*WBP*, 23–28). Modern religion is less and less a matter of authoritative Law and more and more a matter of self-expression.

*A World beyond Politics?* should also be read in conjunction with Manent's masterwork of political philosophy, *The City of Man*.[6] It builds on, but also subtly corrects, that work. In *The City of Man* Manent explores the paradoxes that define modern freedom. In particular, he attempts to make sense of the following paradox: Modern man speaks about nothing but the rights of man but has little to say about who the human being is who bears rights. Manent sets out to provide a phenomenology of modern consciousness that traces the roots of those abstractions, such as History, Society, and economy, that dominate the thought and action of modern humans. The book is most successful as an exploration of the modern philosophical effort to create a new conception of human freedom that escapes from the rigorous demands of both nature and grace. The modern human being is a being in flight, who flees every "heteronomous" demand, every law that restricts his self-creation. But if *The City of Man* wonderfully captures the aspiration of philosophical modernity to create a world beyond nature and grace, it tends to overstate the practical success of this project. *The City of Man* is

5   Manent, *An Intellectual History of Liberalism*, translated by Rebecca Balinski, with a foreword by Jerrold Seigel (Princeton, N.J.: Princeton University Press, 1994).
6   Manent, *The City of Man*, translated by Marc A. LePain (Princeton, N.J.: Princeton University Press, 1998).

marred by a tendency to treat the contemporary world as a mere epiphe-nominalization of the modern project. As a result, several reviewers mis-construed the intent of the book. They read it as a total critique of modernity and assumed that Manent rejected liberal modernity *tout court*. In my view, *The City of Man* and *A World beyond Politics?* must be read in conjunction with each other to adequately appreciate the amplitude, sub-tlety, and prudence of Pierre Manent's reflection on modernity. Together, those two contemporary classics provide the fundamental element of his phenomenology of modern politics.

## The Specter of Depoliticization

In Pierre Manent's view, a specter is haunting Europe, the specter of "hu-manitarian depoliticization," of a project that wishes to say "farewell to pol-itics." More generally, the Europe under construction since the late 1940s is defined by a debilitating ambiguity. European elites cannot decide if they wish to build a new political form that can take its place among the powers of the world, offering itself as ally and rival to the United States, Russia, and China, or whether they wish live in a world without politics—a world that is "immediately human" (*WBP*, 199). In recent years, the balance has shifted in the latter direction. Manent believes that Europe, as presently constituted, undermines the vitality of the old nation-state without establishing a new political form to take its place. The emerging Europe is undoubtedly an eco-nomic and humanitarian presence on the world stage. Lamentably, it is only marginally a collective political actor. This quest for a world without medi-ations or politics runs deeper than the functionalist ambitions of the archi-tects of the post-World War European project. To be sure, designers of the European project, such as Jean Monnet, wanted to build supranational Eu-ropean institutions and structures that would undermine the capacity and will of European peoples to make war on each other. But even more funda-mentally, the economistic and humanitarian features of the emerging Euro-pean community are rooted in the nature or logic of modern democratic life. As Manent writes, "Modern humanity is impatient with regard to all mediations" (*WBP*, 199). We perceive politics as an external and oppressive imposition, one that gets in the way of the "authenticity" or "immediacy" of human experiences. For example, we want our politicians to be direct, to display "immediate, common, natural, informal humanity" (*WBP*, 200). As Manent perceptively observes, we like them to be "cool" and "compassionate" (*WBP*, 200). They must display their common humanity; they must "feel our pain." The ostentatious search for democratic informality unites such otherwise diverse politicians as Bill Clinton, Tony Blair, Lionel Jospin, Jacques Chirac, and figures closer to home. They all aim to be in touch with humanity as such, however clumsily or insincerely.

But without a vital public realm—and in Europe that means self-governing nation-states—there is no way for the various experiences of life to communicate, no way for human beings to make a whole of their lives and aspirations. Only in a political order can the different experiences of life learn to communicate with each other and fruitfully overcome their tendency to become "the sole, immediate and absolute" (*WBP*, 202) criteria of human existence. But by separating the various spheres of life (on page 13 Manent highlights six distinct "liberal" separations including the separation of powers, division of labor, separation of Church and State, separation of civil society and state, and the "methodological" separation of facts and values), a liberal order prepares democratic man to reject the mediation that is the liberal state. Each value, each sphere, wishes to actualize itself on its own terms. But human beings cannot live without an experience of the whole; we naturally desire to unite the various realms of human existence. Totalitarian ideologies promised to restore the political unity of the human race through a "superpoliticization" or overpoliticization (*WBP*, 202) of human life that ended by destroying politics as well as the integrity of the various goods of life. Liberal humanitarianism promises access to human unity without the intercession of politics: morality, law, and commerce unite people without the external restraints that limit freedom and risk the outbreak of war. Manent's book is framed by its critique of those two false solutions to democracy's discontents. His book contains one of the best contemporary analyses of the failure of modern intellectuals adequately to come to terms with the totalitarian experience that dominated the politics of the twentieth century. And it makes clear that "humanitarian depoliticization does not have a more livable endstate than the totalitarian superpoliticization of the twentieth century" (*WBP*, 202). *A World beyond Politics?* can be understood as a (qualified) defense of that fragile historical achievement, liberal politics, against the temptations of both ideological and soft despotism.

Manent believes that the humanitarian project is finally a chimera, that it cannot sustain a livable or truly human world. But the "realism" of the project is attested to by certain "grand developments" (*WBP*, 203) in modern life that seem to support the view that it is possible for human beings to live together without the mediation of politics. Commerce, as Friedrich Hayek, among others, suggested, reveals the possibility of a "spontaneous" human order where human beings are connected by mutual interest and without any explicit political command. "Commerce is the profession of equal men," as Montesquieu said, individuals for whom all the world is a market. The vision of a global commercial society was the great hope of eighteenth-century "commercial republicans" such as Hume and Montesquieu: this vision of globalization has become the lived reality of our time.

Manent devotes two chapters to the "empires" of morality and *droit* (law and rights). Modern people feel "similar" to all other human beings. They increasingly define themselves in terms of purely human relations—relations that do not respect the accident of national distinction. Europeans have discovered the "rights of judges" who punish violators of human rights independently of constitutional forms or national sovereignty. For example, a Spanish judge attempted to extradite and try General Augusto Pinochet for crimes against humanity independently of the wishes, sovereignty, or civic peace of the Chilean people. Judges in Italy (through the anticorruption "Clean Hands" operation) brought down a political order with little concern for the self-government of the Italian people (*WBP*, 186–87). The spiritual power (the phrase was that of the Saint-Simonians) of judges—so contemptuous of political forms—is based "upon the rights of man which have an immediacy to every human being" (*WBP*, 186, with the translation slightly modified). Under the empire of *droit*, any exercise of prudence is a threat to the authentic realization of rights. To be truly affirmed, rights must escape political articulation altogether.

Humanitarian moralism is another substitute for political reason. Humanitarian interventions are increasingly justified in abstraction from any prudential or political considerations. But Manent demonstrates that pity or compassion needs political articulation if it is not to become a self-destructive substitute for political action. Otherwise, it gives rise to incoherent and often tepid displays of moralism. We saw a massive outpouring of humanitarian moralism in response to the Russian invasion of Ukraine in the late winter of 2022. Political judgment gave way to moralism inseparable from political Manicheanism and war fever. In the Kosovo intervention of 1999, the allies could not decide between saving lives or avoiding the death of a single one of their soldiers. Both were legitimate humanitarian aims. In the effort to avoid allied casualties, NATO forces bombed Serbia from such great elevations that they ended up killing thousands of innocent Serbian civilians. Such is the perverse logic of humanitarianism.

Likewise, the appeal to human dignity has lost any substantive connection with the moral law, as it had for Kant, and has become a justification for "respecting" any lifestyle choice or commitment, no matter how odious or idiosyncratic. When human dignity becomes confused with mere relativism, it subverts the liberal order and corrupts the integrity of moral choice. Without making himself a preacher of prudence, Manent highlights the need for a standard of judgment that can weigh and balance the various spheres of life. Without political mediation, each experience imperiously seeks to become the sole measure of human existence. When law, rights, and morality become hegemonic they subvert themselves and undermine the delicate equilibrium of separation and unity that defines a liberal political community. In a word, political reason is indispensable for resisting the totalitarian and humanitarian subversion of free political life.

## The "Nature" and "Art" of Democracy

Like Manent's previous writings, *A World beyond Politics?* contains a sustained reflection on democratic individualism. In Manent's view, the "effectual truth" of the democratic project is the assertion that man is the "sovereign author of the human world" (*WBP*, 157). As Kant argues in *What Is Enlightenment?* modern man has attained maturity only by coming to see himself as self-legislating, only by refusing to serve any natural or divine law that transcends his will (*WBP*, 157). At its deepest level, democracy is the means by which modern humans put in work this project of human sovereignty. In two crucial chapters, entitled "Declaring the Rights of Man" and "Becoming an Individual," Manent traces the way in which the project for human sovereignty creates the modern individual, the individual who affirms his rights against every external or "heteronomous" constraint. The rights of man are the practical instrument of human sovereignty or autonomy. They are the shared reference points for all the intellectual tendencies in the contemporary world. But despite the obligatory appeals to diversity and "difference" in advanced intellectual circles, the emphasis on rights creates an increasingly homogenous world—a world where every institution and claim is beholden to the consent of the individual. When consent becomes the sole principle of the human world, it risks becoming a new source of tyranny. Manent shares, renews, and deepens some of Tocqueville's forebodings about the dangers of democratic or soft despotism.

Under the democratic dispensation, the human person is increasingly transformed into an "individual." Human ties or bonds are fully legitimate only to the extent that they are freely chosen. At the time of the great democratic revolutions of the late eighteenth century, rights still had a recognizably political inscription. Rights belonged to citizens and were tied to the fulfillment of certain civic obligations. But today rights have "an incontestably antipolitical accent" (*WBP*, 99). Collective constraints tied to citizenship, such as compulsory military service, are no longer seen as a crucial means for supporting the political community that guarantees rights. Rather, such measures are said to restrict the free choice of the individual and are thus believed to be incompatible with individual freedom. Manent stresses the ambition of democratic ideology to "voluntarize" all human relations. Not only are rights increasingly shorn of any real political inscription but consent, individual choice, comes to define "the majority of human actions" as Tocqueville put it in volume I of *Democracy in America*. The family, the nation, and the Church, every traditional source of authority and identification, are increasingly redefined in light of the categorical imperative of individual choice. The law no longer recognizes the father as the head of the family. Children are increasingly understood to be equal, at least in principle, to their parents. The contemporary democratic family strives to be as egalitarian and antihierarchical as possible. As I have just noted, democratic nations find it increasingly difficult to require citizens to serve in the armed forces or to ask of them the ultimate sacrifice. That task is left to volunteers who are supposed to risk death as a "professional hazard." And religion has become increasingly therapeutic in character, more a question of personal identity and individual choice than a matter of obedience to divinely constituted authority. Democracy, shorn of the moderating effects of salutary tradition, turns the human world upside down.

Manent thus appears to sketch the outline of a tragedy. Democracy has a "nature" that will not rest until individualism reigns supreme in the social and political world. But this reading, true as far as it goes, risks missing the subtlety of Manent's analysis. As Mona Ozouf has written, Manent is not only a penetrating analyst of the atomizing effects of the democratic project, he is also a "natural friend of conciliation."[7] As Ozouf suggests, Manent wishes to reconcile the "nature" and "art" of democracy with each other. If Manent's writing as a whole tends to suggest that individualism is the effectual truth of democratic social life, *A World beyond Politics?* provides a salutary self-correction. I will briefly sketch the way in which Manent affirms the revolutionary effects of modern individualism as well as the intrinsic limits of the "autonomy project."[8]

Without doubt, Manent sees an element of truth in the conservative, counterrevolutionary, and Marxist critiques of democratic individualism. He is the furthest thing from a complacent liberal. He is less impressed with the antiliberal attacks on the "egoism" of bourgeois society (in his view egoism is an eternal temptation of the human heart) than by their emphasis on the "separating" or "disassociative" propensities of a political order built upon the idea of human rights. In a chapter entitled "Declaring the Rights of Man" Manent confronts the critique of democratic individualism leveled by Marx in his 1844 essay "On the Jewish Question" as well as the criticism of that critique by the contemporary French political philosopher Claude Lefort. Manent chooses to concentrate on the Marxist critique of liberalism precisely because Marx shares and even radicalizes the democratic project's commitment to human emancipation. Manent has no illusions whatsoever about the utopianism of Marx's dream of a postpolitical world without divisions or conflicts, but he is convinced that the Marxist critique of rights can contribute to clarifying the individualist logic of the democratic regime.

7    See Mona Ozouf's eloquent review of *Cours familier* in *Le Nouvel Observateur*, 20 décembre 2001, p. 132.
8    The phrase is from George Weigel's article "A Better Concept of Freedom" in *First Things*, March 2002, p. 17.

Claude Lefort (1924–2010) is one of Manent's principal interlocutors in *A World beyond Politics?*. Not as well-known as he should be in the United States, Lefort is one of the great political philosophers of the age and one of the deepest analysts of democracy and totalitarianism. An ex-Trotskyite, Lefort wrote a magisterial work on the political philosophy of Machiavelli, lucid reflections on the "indeterminacy" of democratic life, and original reflections on such diverse figures as La Boétie, Leo Strauss, Hannah Arendt, Alexis de Tocqueville, and Aleksandr Solzhenitsyn.[9] He is also one of the surest guides to the theory and practice of communism. Manent's examination of the totalitarian temptation is heavily indebted to Lefort's analysis of totalitarianism as a political response to democratic indetermination. But Manent and Lefort part company on the question of rights. Manent is particularly critical of Lefort's effort to affirm the essentially social character of the rights of man. In his essay "The Rights of Man and Politics," found in his 1981 collection *L'invention démocratique*,[10] Lefort takes Marx to task for not appreciating that "bourgeois" rights such as freedom of opinion presuppose communication and exchange—that they do not necessarily lead to the radical atomization of society, as Marx suggests in "On the Jewish Question." Manent readily agrees that Marx overstated the atomizing effects of bourgeois freedom—democratic man is not simply a "monadic individual." But in Manent's view, Lefort is too sanguine about "the connecting effects of the rights of man" (*WBP*, 108). Lefort is confident that the new rights that have proliferated since the 1960s both free the individual from coercive restraints and bring people together in a community dedicated to new articulations of rights. But, in truth, those "new rights" have an almost exclusively corrosive or liberating effect, depending on one's point of view. No-fault divorce, the right to abortion, children's rights, and one could now add transgenderism and the pseudo-rights that flow from it, all follow from

9    Lefort is the author, most notably, of *Le travail de l'oeuvre Machiavel* (Paris: Gallimard, 1972), *L'invention démocratique: Les limites de la domination totalitaire* (Paris: Fayard, 1981) and *La complication: Retour sur le communisme* (Paris: Fayard, 1999). For a representative selection of Lefort's writings in English translation, see Lefort, *The Political Forms of Modern Society: Bureaucracy, Democracy, Totalitarianism*, edited and introduced by John B. Thompson (Cambridge, Mass.: MIT Press, 1986).

10   *L'invention démocratique*, 45–83.

and reinforce an atomizing and individualistic logic (*WBP*, 108–09). Whatever the limits of Marx's positive human vision, whatever his responsibility for the rise of totalitarianism, there is something "profoundly true" in his analysis of modern liberty as the liberty of an "isolated monad" (*WBP*, 109).

Despite their other differences, Marx's analysis in this regard dovetails almost perfectly with Tocqueville's description of "individualism." However, Manent notes that Tocqueville's critique of individualism is more balanced and markedly less ideological than Marx's. His luminous discussion of individualism captures a danger inherent in the nature of democracy. Democratic man is prone to a sentiment "that disposes each citizen to isolate himself from the mass of those like him and to withdraw to one side with his family and friends, so that after having thus created a little society for his own use, he willingly abandons society at large to itself" (*WBP*, 110).[11] But Tocqueville does not ignore the enhanced appreciation of common humanity that accompanies the rise of democratic individualism. He does not argue for the moral superiority of aristocratic man to democratic man. Nor does he ignore the capacity of democratic citizens to correct the individualist propensities of democracy through the political art, through the exercise of democratic self-government. Tocqueville primarily had in mind the local self-government and "art of association" that he saw prodigiously at work in the United States. Manent believes that the nation served an analogous function in modern Europe: it gave a political inscription to rights, it prevented democratic men from escaping from political life altogether. The decline of the vigor of the European nation-state reinforces the depoliticizing and atomizing "nature" of democracy. It confirms the worst fears of both the reactionary and the revolutionary critics of liberal democracy.

In *A World beyond Politics?*, Manent avoids conservative pessimism not only because of his attentiveness to the fecund art of democracy but also because of what we have called his appreciation of the ultimately unrealizable character of the autonomy project. In *The City Of Man* and his 1995 essay "On Modern Individualism" Manent seemed to suggest that the tragic

---

11  I have quoted from the excellent translation of *Democracy in America* by Harvey C. Mansfield and Delba Winthrop (Chicago: University of Chicago Press, 2000). The quotation appears on page 482 of their edition.

fate of modern man was to become more and more of an individual.[12] In *A World beyond Politics?*, Manent qualifies the claim. He eloquently criticizes the tendency of modern philosophers, sociologists, and historians to exaggerate the heterogeneity of the old and the new, the democratic dispensation and what came before it. These contrasts, he writes, tend to be overdrawn. In a remarkably suggestive passage, Manent writes the following:

> There is indeed a polarity between community and authority on one side, the individual and freedom on the other. . . . At the same time, each pole contains the other, normally subordinated but present and at work, and capable of seizing the upper hand. In the old order, community membership was primary and by right, but it was unthinkable without the mediation of consent, which was generally presupposed. Obedience to the king presupposed an interior movement of allegiance, possibly even an explicit and formal oath. Marriage in Christian Europe had always rested in principle on consent, since consent constituted the very substance of the sacrament of marriage. And to take the most indicative example in this context, when the church took unto itself the right to impose the rule of faith, she still affirmed that the act of faith was valid, "meritorious," only when it was freely and sincerely formed.
>
> In the new democratic order, free personal searching is now a right, but it can lead to deep and lasting adherences, whether be it the formation of a couple or participation in a religious or other type of community. (*WBP*, 117).

Manent refuses to jettison either theoretical clarity about the nature of democracy or faith in the sempiternal prospects for human community and fidelity. The notion of pure freedom or consent is a chimera; even worse, it undermines the very possibility of commitment, the very desirability of keeping one's promises. Sartrian freedom, celebrating indeterminate choice,

---

12  See "On Modern Individualism" in *Modern Liberty and Its Discontents*, 151–59, especially page 154. The essay originally appeared in the summer 1995 issue of *Commentaire*.

demands the continuous re-creation of the world—it entails the dissolution of a recognizably human world (*WBP*, 118). It presupposes a world without faith or hope or love. Because the democratic order allows one to choose freely, and even to choose what is genuinely choiceworthy, it is an order to which we owe some gratitude.[13] However, the democratic order also entails a temptation; it tempts us to value choice above "the order of truth" or the nature of things. In any case, human beings are not free to choose between freedom and truth since both are constitutive of our nature. We are destined to live within the order of separations, but we cannot allow these separations to completely rule our minds and souls. We are obliged to live freely but in light of the truth. Such is the art of conciliation.

## Politics and War

One of the most important theoretical contributions of Manent's work is its treatment of political forms. Confronted by the rise of new kinds of tyranny in the twentieth century, political science rediscovered the classical notion of *politeia* or regime. Manent follows both Leo Strauss and Raymond Aron in arguing for the primacy of the political regime. The political regime establishes the authoritative institutions of society and sets the tone of civic and social life. During the "short" twentieth century, which lasted from 1914 to 1989, from the shot fired at Sarajevo that killed the Archduke Franz Ferdinand and triggered the First World War, to the final implosion of the Soviet empire, the triangular conflict between liberal democratic, fascist, and communist regimes and ideologies defined the stakes of universal history. But Manent insists that the regime crucially presupposes a political form, such as the city, empire, or nation. The city is the "starting point of any political reflection" (*WBP*, 44) in the Western world and was presupposed as the natural framework for political life by classical political philosophy. But it does not exhaust the political forms that enframe and give flesh to the political regime.

In "The Question of Political Forms" Manent argues that there are a "pre-determined number of political forms" (*WBP*, 44), that political life must unfold within the framework of either the city, empire, or nation.

---

13   Pierre Manent, interview with Claude Aubert, *Valeurs Actuelles* (11 janvier 2002): 61.

This, he suggests, is "one of the most important 'theoretical' contributions of political science" (*WBP*, 44). This insight has immense practical implications. "If we [Europeans] decisively leave the national form, we shall have to enter another form for one cannot continue to live politically in an undefined way" (*WBP*, 44). Manent brilliantly demonstrates that the classical city was inseparably tied to both liberty, the self-government of (a limited group of) citizens, and to war, both against other cities and between the few and the many within the city. The creation of the modern nation was intended to universalize the civic freedom of the classical city without replicating its potentially suicidal martial tendencies. All these themes would be even more richly developed in Manent's 2013 book (2010 for the original French), *Metamorphoses of the City: On the Western Dynamic* which we have already discussed in chapter two of the book.

The national form was defined, however, by a crippling ambiguity that led it to repeat the oscillation between liberty and war that undermined the utility of the city as a political form. The nation indeed provided the crucial framework for citizenship or democratic self-government, but it was also open to nationalist self-assertion. The Germanic conception of the nation, first articulated by Johann Gottlieb Fichte in his *Discourses to the German Nation* (1807–08), increasingly severed the nation from its universalist aspirations to self-government and human rights. As Ernst Renan famously argued in a letter to David Strauss written in 1871, it risked the outbreak of cruel and limitless "zoological wars" (*WBP*, 79). The wars of the twentieth century would further discredit the nation and would give rise to the illusion that Europeans could live in "civilization," in a merely social and economic community, without choosing among the limited number of political forms.

Politics and war are inseparable in the order of human things. But "advanced" European opinion has come to believe that war is an anachronism. European elites would rather condemn than analyze the wars of the twentieth century. In contrast, Manent argues that "only the effective construction of a political Europe . . . would prove that Europeans have spiritually overcome the intimidation of war" (*WBP*, 72). Quasi-pacifist, humanitarian Europe remains a prisoner of its fear of war and therefore a victim of its history. This is an abdication, an irresponsible display of wishful thinking: "The Europeans of the European Union, the Europeans of 'advanced Europe,' do not have the leisure to unilaterally declare that 'war is finished.' As much as they might want to banish war to a definitely resolved past, they must understand that, in [Charles] Péguy' s phrase, 'military realities have an importance of the first order'" (*WBP*, 72).

Manent reminds us that the hope or expectation for the end of history, for a definitive exit from politics and war, predates the tragedies of the twentieth century. Nineteenth-century liberals, positivists, and Marxists alike had proclaimed the transition from military to industrial society, from a bellicose age to a commercial one. In his beautiful 1814 essay *The Spirit of Conquest and Usurpation*, the great French liberal Benjamin Constant declared the wars of the revolution and empire, as well as Napoleonic despotism, to be an anachronistic residue from the age of conquest and usurpation. And August Comte, the prophet-philosopher of "the religion of humanity," announced in 1841 that "All truly philosophical minds must easily recognize, with perfect intellectual and moral satisfaction, that the age has finally come when serious and sustained warfare must totally disappear among the elite of humanity" (*WBP*, 73).

Manent does not share the extravagant hope of those who believe that war can be eliminated rather than minimized and placed under prudent political direction. If Europeans are going to minimize the incidences and scope of violence, they must first make the requisite effort to understand war. In "The Wars of the Twentieth Century," Manent provides a masterly account of the "wars in chain reaction" (the phrase is Raymond Aron's) that destroyed the self-confidence of the national form and gave rise to the Nazi and communist behemoths. Drawing on the writings of Raymond Aron and Charles de Gaulle, Manent investigates the causal role of war in the drama of the twentieth century. Aron argued that "hyperbolic" war was itself the principal cause of the events that destroyed the old Europe and allowed "abstract hatreds" (*WBP*, 80–83) and totalitarian regimes to dominate the first half of the twentieth century. In *La discorde chez l'enemmi*, his 1924 book on the causes of Germany's defeat in World War I, the young de Gaulle suggested that a principle of corruption or immoderation within the Imperial German regime (which de Gaulle attributed to popularized "Nietzscheanism") led to the reinstitution of unlimited submarine warfare in January 1917 and thus forced the hand of President Woodrow Wilson. Those differing, if complementary, analyses illustrate what it means to think about war. War is itself a product of moral and political passions and ideas, as well as the cause of new political facts. Today Europeans would prefer not to think about war, seeing such reflection as a moral fault, an endorsement or validation of inhuman deeds. But without searching reflection on war and its place in the human order of things, Europeans will remain prisoners of their past. They will remain captive to the destructive illusion that it is possible to leave behind history, a history which "writes its letters in blood"[14] as Raymond Aron put it in the conclusion of his magisterial book on Clausewitz.

## The Totalitarian Temptation

In a remarkably suggestive essay called "The Return of Political Philosophy," published in *First Things* in May 2000, Manent lamented the failure of contemporary political philosophy genuinely to come to terms with the experience of totalitarianism. No major political philosopher of the twentieth century had succeeded in conveying "to the few and many alike a powerful vision of our social and political dynamics,"[15] including the totalitarian regimes and ideologies that ravaged the twentieth century. "Totalitarianism was the *experimentum crucis* for political philosophy in our century. Through it political philosophy was radically tested, and was found wanting."[16] The most impressive documents for understanding National Socialist and communist totalitarianism were in fact written by literary figures such as Orwell, Solzhenitsyn, Zinoviev, or Jünger. Works such as *1984, One Day in the Life of Ivan Denisovich*, and *On the Marmor Cliffs* allow their readers to imaginatively grasp the surreality of ideological totalitarianism. They give readers direct access to a world that needs to be directly experienced to be fully understood. It is true that a few major political thinkers such as Hannah Arendt and Raymond Aron made heroic efforts to confront totalitarianism head-on, and their writings are indispensable for an adequate consideration

14  Raymond Aron, *Clausewitz: Philosopher of War* (Englewood Cliffs, N.J.: Prentice Hall, 1985), 411.
15  Pierre Manent, "The Return of Political Philosophy" in *First Things* (May 2000): 15–22. The quote is from page 15.
16  Ibid., 17.

of the subject. Manent pays tribute to and builds on their admirable efforts.[17] In *A World beyond Politics?* he dedicates two impressive, synthetic chapters, "The Question of Communism" and "Does There Exist a Nazi Mystery?" to a reconsideration of totalitarianism. He sets out to correct this debilitating deficit at the heart of contemporary political philosophy.

In those two chapters, Manent joins thinkers, such as Arendt, Solzhenitsyn, Aron, and his friend, the French philosophical historian Alain Besançon, who have emphasized the ideological roots of both Nazi and communist totalitarianism. Their approach contrasts with the mainstream of Western social science, which tends to view ideology as mere rationalization and which dismisses totalitarianism as a value-laden concept of Cold War inspiration. Undeterred by these criticisms, Manent firmly adheres to the ideological school. It is the ideological desire to create a "new man" and build a new society that accounts for the singular brutality of Leninist communism and the insane social projects, such as the forced collectivization of agriculture, that took the lives of tens of millions of ordinary people in Stalinist Russia and Maoist China. An economically counterproductive project such as collectivization made no sense from a strictly utilitarian or pragmatic point of view. The active persecution of believers, so destructive of social peace and morals, is another consequence of the ideological impulse to build socialism. Likewise, Nazism's murderous project to create a *Juden-frei* Europe is rooted in a profoundly anticapitalist and anticommunist ideology. The hatred of the Jews provides the faux universalist element of Nazi particularism, the key for building a new society that overcomes bourgeois and socialist universalism (*WBP*, 169). Anti-Semitism allowed the Nazis to elicit some support, no matter how limited and misguided, outside of the confines of the German "race."

Like Solzhenitsyn and the authors of *The Black Book of Communism*, Manent does not hesitate to compare and to equally condemn Nazi and communist theory and practice. He in no way denies the uniqueness of the Holocaust, a product of intentional, brutal, and murderous criminality, nor does he allow this uniqueness to excuse communist criminality. He does, however, take the German historian Ernst Nolte to task, not for comparing and identifying the twin totalitarian monsters of the century but for using

17 Ibid., 17–18.

that comparison to relativize Nazi criminality. For Nolte, Nazism is in large part a defensive reaction to the Bolshevik threat. Manent does not deny that there is a "mimetic" dimension to the relationship between communist and Nazi totalitarianism. Lenin was the political and intellectual architect of murderous totalitarianism in the twentieth century. It was Lenin who put forward the first grand vision of ideological social engineering, who reduced "class enemies," such as believers, "kulaks," aristocrats, and independent intellectuals, to "harmful insects" (*WBP*, 158) who needed to be purged from the Soviet lands. All subsequent totalitarianism would follow this pattern of verbal dehumanization followed by incarceration and even physical extermination. But Nolte goes much too far in reducing Auschwitz to a mimetic reflection of and defensive response to the Gulag. Manent trenchantly comments that "It is frankly absurd to suggest that the Nazis killed because they felt directly threatened by the Bolsheviks and so they themselves would not be killed. It is to take the rationalization of the criminal for the explanation of the crime" (*WBP*, 165).

Manent builds on the ideological school but brings political philosophy to bear on its insights and conclusions. As a result, he does justice both to the new and unprecedented aspects of totalitarianism and to its place within the broad movement of modernity. In doing so, he draws particularly on the insights of Alain Besançon and Claude Lefort. Manent's interpretation of communist totalitarianism is best seen as a synthesis of Besançon's analysis of "ideocracy" and Lefort's account of the intrinsic vulnerability of democracy to the totalitarian temptation. In a remarkable 1976 essay entitled "The Difficulty of Defining the Soviet Regime,"[18] Besançon established that neither Aristotle's nor Montesquieu's classifications of regimes could account for the distinctiveness of the Soviet regime. The Soviet regime incorporated oligarchical, despotic, and democratic traits in an unprecedented way. It claimed to govern in the common interest even as it gave rise to a radically new form of tyranny. Only ideology can account for the confusion of categories, for the alluring falsification of the good, which defined communist totalitarianism. In Besançon's account, ideology is the "end and

18  Besançon's article was originally published in *Contrepoint*, #20 in 1976, and was republished in his *Présent soviètique et passé russe* (Paris: Hachette-Pluriel, 1980).

principle of the regime,"[19] and totalitarianism its instrument and means. Manent fully endorses this reading of the "ideological regime."

But, in Manent's view, the ideological regime is made possible by certain profound tendencies within modernity itself. Two quintessentially modern ideas, "the idea of the political order as artifice and supreme instrument, the machine of machines, and the idea of man as a historical being" (*WBP*, 151–52) provide the crucial presuppositions for creating the new man of communist ideology. These ideas have their roots in the non-totalitarian political philosophies of Hobbes and Rousseau, respectively. And the indetermination of democratic society, powerfully highlighted by Lefort in *L'invention démocratique* (Gallimard, 1981), creates a spiritual vulnerability that allows ideology to gain a foothold and unleash its work. Here Manent makes excellent use of Lefort's analysis. The French and European *ancien regime* was a profoundly corporate order, made up of innumerable little bodies by which the people could take their bearings. But democracy "disincorporates" society. In place of the King's visible body, there is only an "empty public space" filled by the changing requirements of representation. Totalitarianism is a natural response to the indetermination that "haunts" democratic society. It is an understandable if perverse effort to reincorporate the social order by affirming collective unity, the "people as One," by attempting to create through revolutionary action a homogenous society without conflicts or divisions. Manent observes that the disappearance of communism leaves the structural problem of democracy wholly intact. There is every reason to suspect that new totalitarian projects will arise in the future, each promising to overcome the indetermination that haunts the democratic order. Manent wisely remarks that these movements may be "more difficult to foresee today as Bolshevism was in 1916" (*WBP*, 160), on the eve of Lenin's return to a war-torn Russia. The perspective of political philosophy thus allows one to see the totalitarian danger in a new light: as both a bastard child of democratic modernity and a radical negation of liberty and human dignity.

Following Leo Strauss, Manent argues that National Socialist nihilism had its roots in a non-nihilistic motive: revulsion at a bourgeois ethic that reduced the human world to the sole imperative of comfortable

19   Ibid., 256.

92

self-preservation.[20] Not without some justice, Nietzsche, Jünger, Heidegger, and their ilk argued that such an understanding was ignoble or unworthy of man. In response to the "bourgeoisifaction" of the modern world, the German radical or atheistic Right, out of which National Socialism developed, turned to the only categorically non-nihilistic motive that they knew, military courage. But militarism eventually gave rise to an ideology of pure destruction, one rooted in the radical rejection of the very ideas of civilization and common humanity. The demonic murder of the Jews was the embodiment par excellence of this rejection of democratic humanitarianism. Communism, on the other hand, radicalized and subverted the democratic impulse. It is therefore a much more dangerous spiritual temptation for democratic intellectuals. Hence the vituperation directed against anyone who compares the crimes of communism with the crimes of National Socialism. Manent's penetrating analysis allows us to see how both radical modernism and vituperative antimodernism can equally give rise to inhuman totalitarianism. His analysis gives powerful support to Raymond Aron's judgment on the two totalitarianisms in his 1965 classic, *Democracy and Totalitarianism*:

> To sum up the meaning of these two undertakings, I think that these are the formulae that I would suggest: for the Soviet undertaking, I would recall the well-known formula: he who would create the angel creates a beast; for that of the Nazi undertaking: man should not try to resemble a beast of prey because, when he does, he is only too successful.[21]

## Summing Up

In *A World beyond Politics?* Pierre Manent has written a genuinely philosophical account of the modern political condition. His book is public

20  In his discussion of the intellectual roots of National Socialism, Manent draws widely on Leo Strauss's magisterial 1941 address on "German Nihilism" that was published posthumously in *Interpretation* and *Commentaire* in 1999.

21  Raymond Aron, *Democracy and Totalitarianism: A Theory of Political Systems* (Ann Arbor, Mich.: University of Michigan Press, 1990), 204.

spirited without ever being partisan or ideological. He draws on the widest range of thinkers, including Rousseau, Marx, and Tocqueville, to illuminate the "problem" of democracy in our time. He artfully unfolds the nature of democracy, its profoundly atomizing tendencies as well as its capacity to re-connect citizens through the art of democratic self-government. His book is a plea for citizens of the Western democracies to cultivate the Sisyphean art by which liberalism finds a political articulation. To contemporary Eu-ropeans who are tempted to leave behind history, to leave behind the world of politics and war, Manent insists on the mediating role of the political regime and the political form. Politics allows human beings "to put in com-mon reasons and actions," as Aristotle beautifully argued in his *Nicomachean Ethics* [1126b, 11–12]. It allows human beings "to act and deliberate to-gether." But contemporary Europe pursues the indefinite expansion of its territory without knowing what it wants to put together. Its elites proceed with the project of "constructing" Europe without paying much, if any, at-tention to the wishes of its citizens. As a result, Europe is suffering from a debilitating democratic deficit. In Manent's judgment, the European project is bound to lead to continued frustration, civic apathy, and international humiliation unless Europeans begin to give serious thought to the political requirements of their project. Humanitarian posturing is no substitute for thinking through one's responsibilities as citizen and statesman.

Manent is aware of the vulnerabilities of the liberal state. He is a chas-tened friend and friendly critic of liberalism; his criticisms of it are lucid and measured. But in *A World beyond Politics?* he also defends the delicate achieve-ment which is the liberal state against its radicalization or subversion. To be sure, the liberal state does not formally recognize the "moral contents of life"; it is largely silent about the highest requirements of the soul. But it allows citizens to distinguish between truth and falsehood; it permits them to pursue the good within the framework of civil society. In contrast, "the politics of recognition" validates relativism as the official philosophy of the state and civil society. "We are asked to respect all the contents of life, all the choices of life, all lifestyles. Now, this formulation really does not have any meaning. Or its sole determinate meaning is that we are asked to approve, to appreciate, to validate, to applaud all the contents of life, all the choices of life, all lifestyles. Now that is simply impossible" (*WBP*, 195, translation revised). In one of the most illuminating and provocative discussions in the book,

Manent presents a compelling liberal argument against the legalization of homosexual marriage, a cogent and compelling argument that was assiduously ignored. In his formulation, homosexuals should be treated with dignity and deserve all the rights accorded free men and women. But a liberal society cannot recognize the homosexual "lifestyle"; it cannot validate it without ceasing to be a liberal state, without subverting its raison d'être. The liberal state can, on the other hand, legitimately "privilege" heterosexual marriage because this marriage, rooted in the "natural division" of the sexes, "produces children, that is, citizens, and that pertains to the *public* interest" (*WBP*, 196). The liberal order ignores human nature, including our biological order, at its peril. Manent renews and deepens this argument in the first chapter of 2018's *Natural Law and Human Rights*. In the fifteen to twenty years between the publication of the two books, the assault on the natural basis of the family, in particular, and of sexual relations, took on the character of a systematic assault, a war on sex in the name of "gender." Confusion reigns supreme.

Like all great works, *A World beyond Politics?* invites the reader to debate its claims as well as its emphases and omissions. I, for one, cannot simply agree with Manent's characterization of America as a (largely benevolent) empire rather than a nation. Of course, America increasingly sets the rules of the international game and dominates international society and the global economy. And American foreign policy does have a very disturbing tendency to collapse the distinction between domestic and foreign matters, to treat the whole world as being, at least in principle, under American jurisprudence (*WBP*, 196). But America is also the world's preeminent example of a self-governing republic. She is the political power par excellence, a clumsy, energetic, imperial nation to be sure.

Pierre Manent wants primarily to understand the world and only secondarily to change it. To understand the world, however, is to appreciate "the humanity of man without illusion, but in the truth of his political nature" (*WBP*, 206). *A World beyond Politics?* is a powerful and profound philosophical response to those on the Left and Right alike who want "to put an end to history, to put an end to wandering."[22] In the spirit of

---

22  See Manent's remarkable "Raymond Aron: Political Educator" in *In Defense of Political Reason: Essays by Raymond Aron,* edited by Daniel J. Mahoney (Lanham, Md.: Rowman and Littlefield, 1994), 22.

Montesquieu, Manent displays a taste and appreciation for the amplitude of the political world; in the spirit of Pascal he displays a rich sensitivity to the paradoxes that define the human soul. In the spirit of Aristotle, he renews the *phronesis* or practical reason, the "God of the lower world," as Burke so suggestively called it. Manent is a true political philosopher because he knows both that human beings will always need "to put in common reasons and actions" and because he has the wisdom to recognize that politics will never fully satisfy our highest aspirations.

# Chapter 6
# TRUTH AND LIES:
# REFLECTIONS ON ROGER SCRUTON'S
# *NOTES FROM UNDERGROUND,* AN ANTI-
# TOTALITARIAN NOVEL PAR EXCELLENCE

Through the publication of *Gentle Regrets* (2005) and *Conversations with Roger Scruton* (2016), we have learned a great deal about Roger Scruton's "work on behalf of the dissidents of Eastern Europe during their communist enslavement," as his interlocutor Mark Dooley puts in the latter of these two works. Scruton has been honored by the governments of both the Czech Republic and Poland for his "intellectual courage and friendship" to both nations during the period of communist captivity. Along with Barbara Day and others, he was a crucial conduit to the intellectual underground in both countries (he was eventually prohibited from returning to Czechoslovakia, as it was then known). *Notes from Underground,* published in English 2014 and in Czech two years later, is, as Dooley puts it, a remarkable and remarkably successful effort "to evoke the strange, threatening and often surreal atmosphere of life under communist rule." And as Dooley also notes, "his experience of those times clearly shaped his consciousness," and I would add his political philosophy, "in an unusual way." It is thus worthy of sustained analysis and reflection.

In the beginning of that work, Scruton observes (in his "Author's Note") that this is a "story about truth" even if most of the characters ("with a few obvious exceptions") "are fictions" (*Notes from Underground,* p. vii, hereafter just the page number). It is an effort to utilize literary art to convey the surreality of an ideological regime founded on lies that are simultaneously ontological, metaphysical, human, and political (or, more precisely, anti-political). Through the organized negation of truth, on a truly systematic and unprecedented level, one (paradoxically) rediscovers the primordial human imperative to "live in truth," to acknowledge that human beings are above all persons to be respected, and not playthings to be endlessly manipulated by ideologues, technocrats, and bureaucrats. The work is set in Prague in 1985, just as the regime of the Lie is to begin its descent into oblivion. And, yet, to almost everyone who lived in this phantasmagorical world, where the meaning of words was seemingly forever lost, it was destined to last forever. Only one character, Betka Palková, sees the end coming, and does her best to prepare for a post-communist future. But, as we shall see, her means of doing so are by no means beyond moral reproach.

The protagonist of the book, Jan Reichl (or "Honza" to use the widely used Czech nickname), is completely alienated from the sordid world of lies surrounding him. He belonged to the "underground" in the literal sense of the term, riding the Prague metro morning and afternoon and observing a world of silence and sartorial conformity that is marked by grayness and the seeming obliteration of human spontaneity. He observes others in their silence but makes no contact with them. He writes up his thoughts in a samizdat volume called *Rumors*, published under the pseudonym "Comrade Underground" (p. 241). This book will ultimately bring him to the attention of the semi-official "underground," the world of long-haired dissidents, underground priests, and unofficial rock bands, as the author puts it. His book will later be praised—by Betka no less—as a masterwork of "phenomenological realism," (p. 239) a true guide to the degraded soul of man under "really-existing socialism." His book was clandestinely published by his mother. She runs a samizdat press, Powerless Press, named after Václav Havel's famous 1979 essay, "The Power of the Powerless," an enduring guide to understanding the nature of the Lie and how a totalitarian or (a decayed and stabilized) post-totalitarian regime makes everyone complicit in the lies and illusions it imposes on the world of common sense and common experience (p. 21). Mother, in her own small way, wished to contribute to the restoration of Reality, of a public world, or *res publica*.

After following a striking young woman to her home, an act of nonconformity if there ever was one, Jan makes the crucial mistake of leaving a copy of *Rumors* on the city bus. In his mind, the woman he followed was indeed Betka Palková, whom we shall hear a great deal more of in the course of our presentation. But this is an illusion that only becomes apparent in the final pages of the book. This mistake leads the secret police, the StB, to his mother's (and Jan's) one-room apartment where his mother produces elegant samizdat volumes from materials illegally provided to her by her employer. Confronted by a policeman, Mrs. Reichl ("Mother") rightly denies all mercenary motives—she does what she does "for love" (p. 3). Her denial is incomprehensible to an agent of a regime which cannot begin to fathom truly higher human motives. As for Jan, whose voice and thoughts inform the narration, *Rumors* has led him "to gain a life" (p. 24). But it also had led his mother to lose one. Such is the drama, so freighted with consequence, that sets this tale in motion.

Early in the book, we learn much about Jan and the Reichl family. His father had initially held out hopes that Czechoslovakia could follow a path of modern "progress." He was not a communist, but a "forward-looking" Left-liberal who soon grew disillusioned with the new order. He was no bold dissident but he took the initiative to organize a reading club where Dostoevsky, Kafka, Camus, and the Czech classics held pride of place. To a thuggish and intellectually corrupt regime, this was interpreted as "subversion in collaboration with a foreign power" (p. 5). Sentenced to five years of forced labor, father ultimately perishes in a mine collapse. The village the family lives in is subjected to socialist reconstruction, an Orwellian term for its thoroughgoing destruction. Relocated to a once beautiful Prague, the family now lives in "an undivided space with a toilet and kitchen" (p. 6) in the soulless housing projects known throughout the communist world.

Mother works in a paper factory and gets paid very little for producing very little—the socialist way, as the narrator notes. Jan and his sister are perceived as ideologically suspect and receive a minimal high school education. His sister proceeds to work in a shoe factory in the Pardubice region; Jan becomes a street sweeper who dreams away amidst very little required work. Jan's discovery of his father's copy of Dostoevsky's *Notes from Underground* allowed him to diagnose his own alienation (p. 8). He now saw the slavery of the Czech people as largely self-imposed, "a disease of the will," "a kind of self-entrapment" where subjects of the invidious tyranny held on to false hopes and "an irrational belief in miracles."

## The Encounter with Betka

Mother's arrest and Jan's encounter with Betka would, however, change everything. Betka, and others such as Father Pavel, will introduce him into the underground "polis" that fragilely persists beneath the negations of the totalitarian regime. The mysterious Betka attempts to return a copy of *Rumors* just after Jan's arrest and immediately discerns that he is "Comrade Underground," the writer/observer who had captured the deep angst of the soul of man under totalitarian socialism. Impressed by the book, she ends up holding on to it. Betka sets in motion contact with figures from the Western embassies, contacts who can help liberate Mother from hopeless anonymity and bring her fate to the attention of the Free World.

The conversations that Jan had with Betka "were the first real conversations" (p. 50) in Jan's life. She was erotically enticing, and sufficiently cultured to discuss literature and music at a high level, even if at first she only listened sympathetically to Jan's discourses about Dostoevsky and Kafka. They had "fallen" into each other's worlds, and Betka uttered his name, "Jan," as if she was "baptizing" him (p. 50). Amidst the spiritual and linguistic degradation all around them, soul met soul. As Scruton has elsewhere observed, things happened like that in that strange, deformed, surreal world. There is no doubt that Jan was utterly enchanted by Betka and that the enigmatic Betka loved Jan, "her "mistake" as she often called him, in her own way. In the coming weeks, they would meet, always at her prompting, at places designated by her and never by Jan. And their erotic encounters occurred in a charming little flat provided to Betka by Vílem, a fellow classical Czech musician with some "official" connections of his own. Initially, Betka insisted that she and Vílem were merely friends. Yet they were more than that. In the privacy of this flat, Betka introduced Jan to official dissident literature, a terrain she was already studying and mapping out in order to become *the* authority on the subject once the madness around them had passed into history.

Betka soon belonged to Jan but, alas, to many other worlds as well. Later we learn that she has a young daughter Olga who is seriously ill. Betka works part-time as a nurse in no small part to get care for her beloved daughter. Betka belongs to many overlapping concentric circles . . . Jan's discovery of new worlds, of an underground that could liberate and not merely reinforce alienation, is coextensive with his encounter with the mysterious if benevolent Betka Palková. This encounter is the heart and soul of the Scrutonian version of *Notes from Underground*.

From the moment that Jan met Betka, she had raised the vital practical question, "What are we going to do with your (Jan's) mother?" (p. 33). Betka, who attempted to live in "the real world" that the communists "abolished . . . long ago," (p. 35) knew that "private criminals," the Winston Smiths of the world, were doomed to harassment, arrest, oppression, and worse. If they did not publicize their deeds, they could perish without anyone knowing their fate. But raising their visibility, she insisted, would raise the cost of crushing them. The "one path to safety" (p. 37) was becoming visible to the West, first to Western embassies, and then to being mentioned on BBC and Radio Free Europe. Being part of a larger public movement such as Charter 77 (which fought for fundamental human and civil rights guaranteed by the Helsinki Agreements of 1975) would be even better. First Betka would make Jan, "Comrade Underground" of his samizdat pamphlet, visible to the entire dissident community. And then Mother's arrest would become a scandal known to informed Western public opinion. Everyone was "massively threatened," as the narrator puts it, and the resort to the Western "human rights machine," as the author rather disparagingly calls it, thus made perfect sense. The problem was that the chief representative of that "machine" in Prague, Bob Helibronn, a press attaché at the American embassy, understood neither the logic of totalitarianism nor the true grounds of resistance to it. He comes across as a cartoon character of sorts, a perfect representative of limitless Western incomprehension about communist totalitarianism.

## Bob Heilbronn or the Incomprehension of the West

Heilbronn's job was to turn the case of every victim of totalitarian repression into a *cause célèbre* in the West. Betka, who seemingly travelled effortlessly between the "official world" and the world of dissidence, knew that there were real heroes among the dissidents—genuinely great people such as Havel, Kanturková, and Vaculík (p. 95). But she saw failures in their midst, too, and not a little boasting and pretense. In some ways, her restrained coolness mixed with unequally restrained sympathy toward the dissidents was marked by cynicism and a faux "realism." Betka seems to lack moral clarity and sympathy for those in grave danger. But she nonetheless did what she could to help Mother by introducing Jan to Heilbronn. For all her compromises, Betka was not ultimately on the side of the oppressors.

Heilbronn could only think (much like contemporary mainstream "political science") in superficial terms about democracy versus dictatorship. Ideological despotism was an insidious tyranny over the body and soul about which Heilbronn, and other sophisticated Westerners, knew nothing. His sociology of the "people's democracies" was both beguilingly simple and beyond simplistic: in his world, there were three classes, "the oppressors, the dissidents, and the silent majority" (p. 106). He failed to see what Havel had taught in his great dissident essays: everyone was complicit in the web of lies at the heart of ideocratic despotism. External coercion was matched by an inner tyranny that suffocated the soul and humankind's natural moral conscience. But Jan, to his credit, saw that real human beings "refused to be categorized" (p. 99). His Dad, who had died at the hands of the regime, was neither "silent" nor a dissident—he attempted to commune with deeper realities through his local reading group. He and his friends found solace in the works of Dostoevsky, Kafka, Camus, and the Czech classics. Mother, with her underground "The Powerless Press," lovingly typed and produced samizdat books (nine *papier-mâché* copies at a time) out of fidelity to her husband and a love of truth. These acts of love were never part of an explicitly political struggle for "human rights." Mother's actions were pre-political, spontaneous revolts against suffocating lies. Jan could not recognize his world in the terrible simplifications put forward by Heilbronn. He protested that "my mother's case is not really about human rights at all" (p. 99). His mother and father were attached to "realities" at the heart of the Czech experience and not to the bloodless political "abstractions" put forward by Heilbronn and his ilk. Where were love, trust, and fidelity in the cold world of "human rights," seemingly shorn of affection and relational duties? How could Heilbronn understand so very little (the same could be asked of the Western journalists and academics as a whole) about the totalitarian assault on the human soul? Of course, this ignorance massively persists.

# Rudolf's Seminar

One of Betka's great gifts to Jan was to introduce him to the official world of dissidence, represented and embodied by Rudolf Gotthart's seminar. The seminar would meet on most Fridays at 6:00 p.m. Surrounded by a conspicuous secret police presence, those committed to the stubborn if fragile reality denied by the ideological world all around them would scatter across the carpet on Rudolf's apartment floor. They whispered greetings and searched for solidarity with other souls in search of truth. Rudolf's seminar was an example of the "parallel polis" theorized by the great Czech Catholic dissident Václav Benda in a famous samizdat essay by that name. It was a "true place of refuge," a "temple where ancestral gods kept vigil over (the) collective soul" (p. 55). On the margins of a decaying totalitarian society, these lost souls found strength and pride and solace in the "solidarity of the shattered."

Jan found spiritual strength in this new setting. He could now come out of the truly subterranean underground where he wrote as "Comrade Underground." Betka was a benevolent presence among Rudolf's dissidents, almost a "guardian angel," who seemed "cool," "calm," and distant in Jan's estimation. In some ways, this new setting, so exhilarating and liberating for Jan, was "nothing special for her" (p. 57). She was a cool cat, a person who reflected fathomless moral ambiguity combined with genuine generosity.

In an earlier private conversation with Jan, Betka expressed reservations about Jan Patočka, the courageous Czech philosopher and phenomenologist who was the first spokesman for Charter 77. He died in 1978 after several intense and grueling interrogations from the StB. Betka could find in Patočka's profound and haunting *Heretical Essays*, published in the West and samizdat, only "pretty unreadable stuff." Jan countered: "he wrote that way because he was wrestling with darkness" (p. 49). Betka somewhat cynically replies that the darkness he was wrestling with was "his own darkness" (p. 49). Rudolf, in contrast, leads his seminar through Patočka's "drastic words," full of philosophical technicalities and "frightening evocations" that announce the destruction of Western civilization. Rudolf rightly sees in Patočka's tragic message a path (and call) to unite sacrifice and freedom. "Out of the prison of the everyday," through the darkness of the enforced Lie, Patočka announces the perennial human duty to "care for the soul," the foundational experience of the true *polis*. Patočka theorized the "solidarity of the shattered" which became a palpable, if ever threatened, reality in the Czech underground (see p. 58 for the aforementioned quotes).

Looking back from his university post in Washington, DC twenty years later, Jan compares the superficiality of democratic freedom, "where friends come and go with easy hilarity and where fear is a specialist product," to the world of the seminar where "friendship had the furtiveness of sin" (p. 58). While Betka is suspicious of an impenetrable darkness at the heart of Patočka's philosophical reflections, Scruton, as Mark Dooley reports in a crucial chapter on Eastern Europe in his indispensable *Conversations with Roger Scruton*, was "very inspired" by Patočka's writings. He even played a small role in bringing it to the West. All of us moderns are, Patočka argued, "fragmented and threatened," not simply those who live under the tyranny of the totalitarian Lie. The need for community and truth are perennial. We are obliged to put ourselves and our polis back together again. Patočka's "care of the soul" beckons all who are not content with the death, or eclipse, of the "ancestral gods." His is a philosophy that speaks to the enduring needs of the soul—and the polis. It is a modern manifestation of Platonic and phenomenological wisdom, of old verities whose truth became self-evident in the struggles of the Czech underground.

Jan Reichl left his first encounter with Rudolf's seminar "as though walking on air" (p. 61). The seminar would become an essential part of his new life where he, too, experienced the "solidarity of the shattered." Through it he would discover those like Karel, the pseudonymous Petr Pius, who would expose "the deep torment of our torment" through brilliant musings on the linguistic "regime of nonsense." Such linguistic tyranny mocked everything that "cannot be bought and sold: Love, honor, duty, sacrifice." Communism, Karel showed, was a "world of falsehood" and "kitsch of a new kind: kitsch with teeth" (pp. 116–17), a truly memorable and evocative formulation. Through the seminar Jan would also meet Father Pavel who, like Betka, opened new and liberating paths of the spirit to him. Scruton, the artful philosopher-novelist, makes the things of the spirit, so fragile in the kingdom of falsehood, palpable. The inner life of totalitarianism, of logocratic or ideological tyranny, comes alive. It is vivified through literary art, and becomes open, as Havel would say, to the truth that inheres in "personal experience."

## The Mystery of Betka

Betka is at the same time the most enticing, luminous, enigmatic, and morally ambiguous figure in *Notes from Underground*. She has made troubling compromises in order to maintain contact with reality in an ideological world marked by pretense and deception. She is cultivated and aloof and will do what she has to do to protect her sick daughter Olga, and to build a future for herself in the coming world beyond communism. Of all the characters in the book, she is most aware that the "kingdom of falsehood" is on the verge of imploding and that new possibilities will emerge for her (and Olga) if only if she begins to prepare the way. She thus accepts the patronage of Vílem and makes deals with unsavory types she despises such as Professor Gunther. Yet she has opened new worlds for Jan and keeps alive a "home" uncontaminated by the mendacity around her. It is not only Jan who has come to love her. The author of *Notes from Underground* is clearly smitten by her capacity, as the narrator puts it, to acquire "a home in the time of our nation's homelessness" (p. 151). Finding and sustaining a home worthy of free and responsible persons is perhaps the Scrutonian theme par excellence. Betka semi-miraculously represents that possibility amidst the rubble of a "political" order (actually no *polis* at all) that has declared war on the very possibility of home.

Betka's spiritual achievement becomes truly luminous in chapters 17 and 18, the central chapters of the book. Betka opens herself up, like never before, by bringing Jan to what was once Czech Sudetenland. Here she has built a home that is impervious to the moral and physical blight all around her. In the train carriage on the way to this furtive home, Jan sees the concentric circles of destruction wrought by a regime that only knows how to negate and tear down. There are desecrated farms where "the indigenous gods had retreated" (p. 141), and scarred hills without trees or grass. Churches and villages were dilapidated and abandoned. What passed for industrial modernism, for socialist "progress," was in fact a dirty, concrete, and polluted world in which the face of the landscape "had been eaten away" (p. 142). But as Betka and Jan approach the old Sudetan

105

countryside, traces of an older, more human and sacred way of life begin to emerge.

## Betka's Home

Jan is taken to a world on the edge of a forest, a world where nature still reveals her beauty, and where the remnants of old peasant homes and peasant churches begin to revivify the senses and the soul. Betka and Jan experience the hospitality of an old woman, Mrs. Nemčova, who greets them with endearments and an old-fashioned hospitality. She clearly loves Betka and is a crucial part of her "home." Living outside the world of the collective farm, Mrs. Nemčova reveals the charms, the "unbought grace of life," as Burke called it, of "a nineteenth-century fairy tale" (p. 144). In this little cottage on the edge of the forest, Jan practiced what Father Pavel called the "gymnastics of attention," taking in the attractions of a peasant world that "stood near the source of Betka's life" (p. 144). Proceeding to Betka's own half-hidden home, Jan would see the tomb-like remains of the "communist war on property," on "the pests" (p. 145), the God-fearing Sudetan peasants who had truly inhabited these lands. Betka tellingly relates how this land "was stolen from the people who made it." Klement Gottwald and his communist thugs led a war against the Czech German peasants, not only for the crimes of Hitler and his minions, but even for the seventeenth-century "Battle of the White Mountain," "when the old Czech nation was destroyed" (p. 146). Betka's own lovely home (her "autarkic kingdom" [p.148]) with its rubble, plaster, oaken tables and chairs, Czech and German books, and upright piano were, sadly enough, the result of a prior dispossession. Her cottage, the remnant of an older and more humane world, had the character of a "shrine maintained, with impeccable taste, to a life that had gone" (p. 149). This is a manifestation of the "sacred," as Roger Scruton understands it, of what is truly holy or blessed, consecrated to the gods, amidst the mundane realities of the temporal world. It is a world touched by grace.

But this shrine, this home would not exist without a founding crime of the most invidious character. Betka relates that her grandfather had come "to this place at the end of the war" (p. 153), the Second World War. He was part of a brutal and chaotic band of partisans who accompanied the victorious Red Army to this part of Czechoslovakia. They murdered and pillaged the people of this land with impunity. The local Czech Germans were forced to wear armbands with the letter N for Nazi. Their land, their homes, their tools, and their animals were shamelessly stolen from them. Men and women who had led blameless lives were held responsible for the crimes of others. Betka describes a brutal "nightmare" where children were mercilessly deprived of their inheritance. The home she had lived in until she set out for Prague at nineteen to pursue her studies was in truth other people's property given to her rapacious grandfather by a cruel and tyrannical Communist regime. In a sense, it was not her home at all. But Betka, in semi-Christian tones, came to see it as a place "entrusted to [her] by suffering" (p. 154). In that sense, it was indeed her home, her trust, surrounded by the tombs of hardy and decent souls whose subterranean presence truly blessed this plot of land.

## Becoming a Disciple of Father Pavel

If Jan's profoundly personal, intellectual, and erotic encounter with Betka opened up for him a new way of relating to himself, others, and the world, his encounter with Father Pavel Havranék is almost as transformative. He met Father Pavel at Rudolf's seminar, the place where "the solidarity of the shattered" manifested itself with a luminous mixture of grace and barely concealed excitement. The fragile men and women whom Jan met at the seminar, all of whom are "massively threatened," refuse the ideological negation of the real. They listen with rapt attention to philosophical, political, literary, and spiritual discussions that allow them to experience once again that they are beings with souls. They experience a kind of underground *polis* where Patočka's "care of the soul" becomes meaningful once again, the only kind of polis possible under conditions of totalitarianism.

Like Betka, Pavel is a mysterious soul; he never reveals the full truth about himself. But he is undoubtedly in touch with the things of the spirit, helping give Jan access to those intimations of the transcendent that can still be experienced at "the edge of things" (to use one of Scruton's favorite expressions). Pavel feels, more deeply than most, the absence of God's presence, what he also calls "the void." But he refuses to succumb to nihilism or unbelief. He sees into "unacknowledged parts" (pp. 190–91) of Jan's soul, piercing through his deeply ingrained Czech skepticism. Where others see the void, Pavel experiences God's silence, which is still a form of grace and revelation. He does his best to convey these mysteries to Jan.

Jan sees in Pavel a "spiritual being" who incarnates a "presence" all his own. Pavel helps Jan to see a holiness, a sacredness, in ordinary things, from a "rough cloth on which to kneel" to the "cracked porcelain cup which served as a chalice" (p. 86) in Father Pavel's underground church. He allows Jan—and the reader—to grasp that there is no yawning abyss separating the natural and supernatural. Both are in some mysterious and ineffable way "one and the same" (p. 86). His message and personal bearing resonated with Jan and allowed him to see "the supernatural as an everyday presence, folded into the scheme of things like the lining of a coat" (p. 86). Pavel saw the truth of the Christian religion in its divestment of power (most imperfectly achieved in a fallen world, of course) and in its willingness to "suffer and forgive" as did Christ the Redeemer. The Son of God is also the Suffering Servant. Father Pavel revealed many such truths to Jan, undermining his skepticism and religious indifference without making Jan a believer. Like Betka, he "did not wish to be entirely known, not even to those he trusted" (p. 93), such as Jan. Jan respected him for this since Pavel's way of relating to those who were close to him "conveyed an experience of the world that had the authenticity of suffering" (p. 93). Like Betka, Pavel touches deep recesses of the soul and puts one in touch with enduring mysteries while being something of a mystery himself.

In a surreal ideological world dominated by a tyrannical logocracy as the Polish poet Czeslaw Milosz helpfully called it, Pavel lived by the truth of Christ's light that is paradoxically revealed in his freely chosen suffering and death. Betka admired Pavel but never forgot that he was a priest who wanted to hear your confession, as she put it, to bring you to the silent God who still calls your name. But Jan literally came out of the underground to the anti-totalitarian polis to which Betka introduced him. With Pavel, too, he went to places that he "had never imagined to exist." He listened to music that could not be openly performed, read books that could never be legally published, and sat in underground churches where courageous men, the clergy of the underground, whispered "old and forbidden" truths. The narrator eloquently highlights the importance of Father Pavel to Jan's discovery of a truth. "Father Pavel, like Betka, knew people with keys to secret places." These keys gave one access, perhaps for the first time, to the real, to the soul, to the "solidarity of the shattered."

The "death of God" is another grand lie or deception since it ignores the things of the spirit that still grace a fallen world where shattered men and women cry out for light and truth. The ideological Lie denies the truth of the person and the truth of a human freedom that finally escapes all determinism and necessity. Paradoxically, through its negation of the Real, it also provides powerful evidence that we continue to live in a world of persons. The best of these will resist, however haphazardly and incompletely, all efforts to define them out of existence. As we have seen, Scruton the critic of totalitarianism is also the critic of every form of scientistic reductionism. As Mark Dooley has written, the person, freedom, and the sacred (understood in a most capacious way), remain the English philosopher's three great *transcendental* features of human experience. This triad cannot be explained away by pseudo-science or scientism or deterministic ideologies that ignore the personal experiences at the heart of the human soul's experience of the world. The more we succumb to what the political philosopher Eric Voegelin has called "modernity without restraint," the more the chilling gap between modern ideology and personal experience becomes humanly untenable. It entails a forced, nihilistic denial of the soul and of the God who reveals himself at "the edge of things." Father Pavel represents or embodies some of Roger Scruton's deepest "personalist" convictions, indebted as they are to the Christian faith, the philosophy of Kant, and the experience of totalitarianism in the twentieth century. In his fictional writings, Scruton conveys the ineffable that is experienced at the edge of things, something which is beyond the capacity of nearly all academic philosophizing. In such literary art, the transcendent becomes truly vivid and personal experience manifests itself in dramatic form.

## The Odious Professor Gunther and the Response of Father Pavel

Father Pavel does more than poetically evoke the presence of a silent God in a world where technique, pseudo-science, and totalitarianism have blocked direct contact with the deepest recesses of the human soul, and the accompanying intimations of Transcendence. He is repulsed by Professor

Martin Gunther, the New York University Professor (with a more than pass-ing resemblance to the legal theorist Ronald Dworkin) who comes to Rudolf's seminar only to lament the repression of "marginalized groups" (minorities, homosexuals, feminists, etc.) and to praise "abortion rights" as the fundamental human right (p. 170). Abortion had been imposed on the peoples of the Eastern bloc as a means of eliminating unwanted children rather than caring for them. The public discussion of the matter was skewed by communist doctrine and the enforced silence of the Christian Churches. Pavel is sickened by what the "human rights machine" in the West has de-fined as fundamental liberties. He sees the rights defended and promoted by Gunther as "the privileges of comfortable people" (p.173) who give little sustained thought to the moral grounds of human dignity. They defend a conception of rights, full of subtle, abstract arguments, that forget the obli-gation of the strong and powerful to do no intentional harm to the weak and vulnerable. Pavel simply cannot abide "impeccable arguments for thinking that the unborn can be disposed of according to our inconve-nience" (p. 173). Father Pavel speaks in a Christian idiom that has not lost touch with the indispensable connections between right, justice, and truth. That connection, at the heart of an older Western and Christian civilization that Pavel still represents, has no meaning for the insidiously clever Gun-ther. But Gunter's soulless conception of human rights, informed by ideo-logical clichés, and bereft of serious moral content, is a portent of a future (Czechoslovakia's post-communist future and the West's increasingly sordid present) where human rights are more or less severed from perennial human obligations, from the experiences that give rise to moral and civic respon-sibility and a truly common world.

In the course of the novel, we learn more about the inner and outer lives of Betka and Pavel, its two most, enigmatic and alluring characters. It turns out that Father Pavel Havranék had served as Betka's parish priest in the old Sudetenland, where Betka had made a splendid home for herself amidst the dislocations of modern Czech life. He had served his congrega-tion from 1969 to 1971, and again between 1975 and 1979, "when pre-sumably arrested and the church was finally closed" (p. 227). And now the narrator brings all the connecting threads together: "Father Pavel was her priest, her mentor, and surely her lover and the father of her child" (p. 227).

Later when Betka goes to New York University and takes up a position at the invitation of the distasteful Professor Gunther, Professor Palková, as she is now known, dedicates her book on the world of Czech dissidence "To Pavel, and in the memory of our dearest Olga." Things here come full circle. To be sure, the coming together of an underground priest and a half-dissident and half-collaborator was not so strange in a world marked by incomprehensible moral ambiguity. These were surreal times that made strange and unfathomable connections possible. We will return to this theme shortly.

## The Edifice Collapses

By now, Gorbachev, the reformist communist, is in power in Moscow, and things begin to change in the eastern satellites. Jan's Mother is home from prison. In this new, comparatively "liberal" atmosphere, Rudolf aspires to emigrate, and Karel, the linguist who so powerfully exposed the *langue du bois*, was "emerg(ing) from his boiler house," the boiler house being a typical fate for so many Czech dissidents who were spared prison terms. Igor (most probably modeled on the Catholic dissident Václav Benda) wished "to be either Pope or President" (p. 230), a rather harsh judgment, one might conclude, despite Benda's unbending self-assurance. In the midst of these new dislocations and emerging hopes, Jan has a new job where he does his best to forget Betka while "making use of all the things" he had learned through her (p. 230).

Prague is soon transformed. The heroic Havel is now President, catapulted by his civic courage, books, and his dissident essays. Tourists are everywhere, as are fast-food restaurants. And, of course, there is that seedy undercurrent of late modernity, pornography. The old Prague of churches and culture, of dissidents and the "solidarity of the shattered," is destined to be eclipsed yet again. The narrator's conclusion is not reassuring: "The slaves had been liberated, and turned into morons" (p. 234). The sparks of the spirit that informed the Underground at its best could hardly become the basis of a free society opened to limitless vulgarity. Democratic mediocrity replaced soulless totalitarianism, an improvement no doubt, but no true ascent of the soul.

There is one curious and disturbing passage near the end of the book that speaks volumes about the soul of the new Prague and the liberated Czech lands. Jan passes a meeting where a person resembling Father Pavel, dressed in a suit, is repeating clichés about "a new kind of politics, an 'anti-politics,' which would permit us to be no longer slaves but citizens, enjoying our freedom and rights." The narrator, Jan in this case, comments acerbically that this speech "could have been scripted by Professor Gunther, so replete was it with clichés, and so far from the mysticism that had wakened in me the frail spirit of discipleship" (p. 232). Who knows if this is really Father Pavel? But undoubtedly Jan's thought that it might be him reflects the new clichés which had replaced the language of soul common to Patočka and Father Pavel. But these slogans are still much better than Gunther's. So too are the linguistic tics of the post-1989 Havel, transforming the elevating analysis of his 1979 essay "The Power of the Powerless" into slogans, still informed by thought that could perhaps, at least minimally, guide, sustain, and elevate a democratic people. Jan's instinctive response to this encounter seems unduly harsh and pessimistic. Reality will always be more prosaic than poetic, as all of us in the "Free World" should already know. It takes spiritual strength not to have mere contempt for the more prosaic aspects of ordinary experience that Heidegger, from his Olympian philosophical heights, called "average everydayness."

The "average everydayness" of bourgeois civilization has its decencies but it is rarely spiritually sublime. There is no "solidarity of the shattered" in the new world of consumerism, ever more insistent rights, and a materialist cornucopia accompanied by public corruption and a drift toward moral nihilism. No wonder that the "dissident experience" has been reduced to clichés about "anti-political politics" and "politics, morality, and civility" (clichés, if we want to call them that, that dominated Havel's public addresses and writings after 1989). Those clichés reflect the real experiences of a polis (of sorts) that had emerged in the underground of a decayed and decaying totalitarian regime. Can some of that experience be passed on to the decidedly unheroic consumer democracy that emerged after the fall of communism? Scruton has his doubts. Such a polis, too, survives, if it is capable of surviving, on the edge of things. There is undoubtedly sadness that accompanies this recognition.

# A Postscript: In America

This book ends, not without a touch of additional sadness, with both Betka and Jan settled in the United States fifteen years after the fall of European communism. Alzbêta Palková has written her widely praised book on the Czech dissident culture. In it, she lauded the heroism of "those forced by their love of books to live in the catacombs" (p. 239), but also highlighted their self-deception. Her austere distance from those dissident struggles remains. She is under the patronage of the hideous Martin Gunther at a New York university that also publishes her book. Betka's book makes generous references to *Rumors* by Soudruh Andros, which is singled out for its "way of combining stark objectivity with a suffering inwardness" (p. 239). This is a beautiful and truthful description, indeed. A single footnote identifies Jan Reichl as the author of the book.

Betka, it seems, has made a conventional home for herself in the American academy. Her sublime intelligence and her preternatural sense of home are hardly needed in a free world where soul rarely meets soul, and where the dangers are superficial. Jan, too, is an academic at (the fictional) Wheaton College in Washington, DC. He was welcomed there in the aftermath of the revolutions of 1989, but no one is now much interested in hearing about a tyrannical world beyond all comprehension, and one from a seemingly distant past. Jan's scholarly publications never came to fruition and he experiences a new solitude where the "bright exterior" (p. 239) of American life conceals the paucity of anything resembling an inner life in the true sense of the term. Dismissed from his job at Wheaton College, Jan receives a package from Betka with the only extent copy of *Rumors* to have survived. If he had looked closely, he would have realized that the copy Betka sent him had the tiny marks in it that he had made before leaving it on a city bus. Betka had not borrowed a copy from Mother, as she claimed. Rather, it had been put in her hands by the police. Her freedom, her flexibility, her mysterious distance from both the dissident world and the official world of violence and lies was made possible by unsavory collaboration with the secret police.

The most luminous figure in this book undoubtedly had many such assignments in the past. On this one, she fell in love with Jan and would henceforth do everything to protect him (and to help Olga get treatment for her illnesses). Betka is drawn to the dissident culture but cannot truly be a part of it. She wants to rise above the sordid reality of totalitarian mendacity but willingly serves the official machine of repression and deception, for reasons we all readily understand. Does working for the secret police negate her obvious grace and independence of spirit, and her love and generosity towards Jan? The author of the book does not seem to think so. But every reader must make this vexing, and not so obvious, judgment for himself. I am inclined to see her moral flexibility as both understandable but, in the end, unsavory and unforgiveable.

## An Anti-Totalitarian Classic of the First Order

Roger Scruton's *Notes From Underground* is in keeping with a small group of classics that truly get to the heart of the totalitarian negation of the real. These are works that deftly combine literature and philosophy, and sometimes theology, too, and speak to the soul as it confronts the demons of modernity. These books include Solzhenitsyn's magisterial *The Gulag Archipelago*, Arthur Koestler's *Darkness at Noon*, and Alain Besancon's *The Falsification of the Good*, which gets to the heart of the totalitarian and ideological project to falsify the Good with the help of George Orwell, the author of *1984*, and Vladimir Soloviev, the great Russian Christian philosopher and theologian. All of these memorable books confront, with rare philosophical depth and a literary art that captures the greatness and misery of the human soul, the capacity of life and truth to resist a nothingness that is surely demonic. To resist the ideological Lie is thus to restore truth—and hope—to their central places in the economy of human things. *Notes From Underground* is an achievement of the first order, a book that deserves to endure.

## Sources and Suggested Readings

All references to Roger Scruton's *Notes From Underground: A Novel* (New York: Beaufort Books, 2014, 2020 for the paperback) are cited internally in the body of the text. In the course of my reflection on this work, I have consulted thoughtful reviews by John O'Sullivan, Flagg Taylor, and Robin

Ashenden that appeared in *The New Criterion*, (March 2014), *Law and Liberty* (July 8, 2015), and at CEEL.ORG.UK (October 7, 2015), respectively.

Michael Zantovsky's elegant reflection ("Message in a Bottle") on the stunning veracity of Scruton's book appeared at *Standpoint* on April 29, 2014.

For helpful background on Scruton's engagement with the intellectual underground behind the Iron Curtain, especially in Poland and the Czech lands, see chapter 5 ("Eastern Europe") of *Conversations With Roger Scruton*, by Roger Scruton and Mark Dooley (London: Bloomsbury, 2016), pp. 65–83). I have cited pp. 65 and 66 and made reference to the discussion of Jan Patočka's works on pp. 77–80.

For an introduction to Jan Patočka's thought, see Erazim Kohák editor, *Jan Patočka: Philosophy and Selected Writings* (University of Chicago Press, 1989); Patočka's *Plato and Europe*, translated by Petr Lom (Stanford University Press, 2002); and Patočka's *Heretical Essays in the Philosophy of History*, translated by Erazim Kohák (Open Court, 1999). The latter work contains the seminal discussion of the "solidarity of the shattered.

Václav Havel's most profound essays, "The Power of the Powerless," and "Politics and Conscience," can be found in Havel, *Open Letters: Selected Writings: 1965-1990*, translated by Paul Wilson (New York: Alfred A. Knopf, 1991), pp. 125–214, and pp. 249–71, respectively. Roger Scruton is the co-translator of "Politics and Conscience," an essay which originally appeared in *The Salisbury Review* in January 1985. These essays contain profound critiques of the ideological Lie and a bracing call for "living in truth." Havel's defense of truth and civility in human and political life takes on a more formulaic character in Havel, *The Art of the Impossible: Politics as Morality in Practice*, translated by Paul Wilson (New York: Alfred A. Knopf, 1997). But the best of these latter essays are still very much worth reading.

Solzhenitsyn's *The Gulag Archipelago* is the most powerful indictment of totalitarianism ever written. In forceful and eloquent prose, it exposes the "lie as a form of existence." Its central sections explore the complex and paradoxical ties between "the soul and barbed wire." This magisterial work does full justice to the claims of both political liberty and the human soul. The best available edition was republished by Vintage in the fall of 2018 (on the 50th anniversary of the book's completion and the centennial of Solzhenitsyn's birth) with a penetrating "Foreword" by Jordan B. Peterson. For a fuller discussion, see Daniel J. Mahoney, "Solzhenitsyn: Politics and the Ascent of the Soul," *Modern Age* (Spring 2019), pp. 17–23.

Roger Scruton played a key role in the publication of an English-language edition of Alain Besançon's *The Falsification of the Good: Soloviev and Orwell*. Matthew Screech's translation of the book was released by Claridge Press in 1994. This powerful if little known work originally appeared in French in 1985. It is a masterpiece of theological-political reflection that, as profoundly as anything ever written on the subject, exposes the demonic nothingness at the center of ideological despotism. The French edition, *La falsification du bien: Soloviev et Orwell*, has been republished in Alain Besançon, *Contagions: Essais, 1967–2015* (Paris: Les Belles Lettres, 2018), pp. 643–785.

# Chapter 7
# THE FACE OF FREEDOM: THE DEFENSE OF THE SOUL IN THE THOUGHT OF ROGER SCRUTON

In the opening chapter of this book, I called Roger Scruton a partisan of "the soul and civilization." I meant that as the highest compliment. Roger understood as well as anyone the essential nobility of civilization and fully appreciated that the alternative to it was nothing less than barbarism. He was at once a lucid and learned defender of our Western inheritance, an advocate of the rule of law in the civic realm and the moral law in the ethical realm, a thoughtful elucidator of the mysterious interpenetration of "time and the timeless" that he called the sacred, and a philosophical student of aesthetics who adamantly rejected the view that beauty was "nothing more than a subjective preference or a source of transient pleasure." Roger Scruton was that rare contemporary philosopher who believed that "reason and value penetrate our lives" and that "for a free being, there is right feeling, right experience, and right enjoyment just as much as right action," as he eloquently put it in the concluding paragraph of his indispensable little book, *Beauty: A Very Short Introduction* (2009).

In this reflection, I would like to give an account of some revealing and illuminating passages from Scruton's most profound and satisfying collection of essays, 1990's *Philosopher on Dover Beach* (presently available in paperback from St. Augustine's Press). If I were to recommend one book by Scruton it would be this one, supplemented by the *Conversations with Roger Scruton* that were so thoughtfully initiated and conducted by Mark Dooley and published by Bloomsbury in 2016, a book that we have had reason to recur to. Together, these works illumine the breadth and depth of the Scrutonian account of the "life-world," his defense, at once philosophical and civic, of personhood, moral agency, and those experiences of freedom and accountability that point toward the reality of the sacred beyond all considerations of utility and evolutionary dogmatism. In these writings, a conservative and philosophical appreciation of the multiple grounds for gratitude coexist with a thoughtful and spirited resistance to every form of reductive materialism and scientism, as well as a fierce yet profound opposition to the totalitarian negation of liberty and human dignity. These are, as we have abundantly seen, the quintessentially Scruton themes.

Let us concentrate on two of Scruton's essays that will surely endure. The first, the title essay "The Philosopher on Dover Beach," is an obligatory starting point for reflection on all things Scrutonian. There, Scruton sympathetically recounts Kant's efforts to provide a "moral basis for religious doctrine," or at least a self-confident affirmation of the moral law that respects the religious impulse. There is little doubt that Scruton's own efforts to sketch a theology that can speak convincingly to modern men and women, owes a great deal to Kant's elementary insight "that morality is the ground rather than the consequence of religion." While Kant largely transformed religious reverence toward God into esteem for the moral law as "the supreme instrument of Reason," Scruton ultimately saw in the face of man an intimation of the face of God, "The Soul of the World" as he later called it in an estimable 2015 book by that name.

Even before his (qualified) return to the Christian faith of which we have had reason to speak, Scruton resisted naturalistic and genealogical accounts of religion and moral phenomena, whether the Nietzschean account of biblical religion as a form of resentful self-abasement, or the utterly misplaced Marxist effort to increase "the power of the powerless" by destroying religion, thus taking "away from the powerless the little power they have." Neither the Nietzschean cause of limitless self-affirmation nor the Marxist cause of Utopian justice rooted in a groundless belief in historical inevitability can sustain a human order marked by civic freedom and moral accountability. As Scruton never tired of pointing out, much twentieth century thought, such as Jean-Paul Sartre's indefatigable support for revolutionary extremism, incoherently combined "absolute lawlessness and [the] unanswerability of the existentialist anti-hero," bereft of enduring moral principles, with the "selfless," if nihilistic, "pursuit of revolutionary justice." As Raymond Aron once wrote, "the two extremes"—absolute lawlessness and

revolutionary justice—meet in a nihilistic voluntarism at the service of fanatical politics. The "two extremes," indeed. In them, we are completely
estranged from moral decency and high political prudence.

Scruton brilliantly saw that the search for redemption through the revolutionary politics of the atheistic Right and the atheistic Left always cul-
minated in self-enslavement and the destruction of civilization and the soul.
The "new morality of Marx and Lenin" led only to "the Gulag and the self-
expanding system of enslavement" which is coextensive with ideological
despotism and mendacity. The "old transcendental faith," as Scruton called
it in this essay, can account for the evils that necessarily flow when the "precious ideas of freedom and responsibility" are driven underground and
"have no public recognition, and no place in the administrative process."
Even before Scruton returned to his more explicit Christian affirmation,
no matter how personal and idiosyncratic, he recognized that "impersonal
(and therefore ungovernable) evil is the true legacy of the naturalistic view
of man."

Vigorously opposing political atheism, Scruton turned to those intimations of transcendence at "the edge of things" precisely because, as a
philosopher and human being, he could not reasonably deny "the divine
spark in man." Scruton came to see that while revolutionary consciousness
of a Marxist-Leninist sort "clothe[d] itself in Utopian ambitions," its willful
negation of the moral law gave fanatical and nihilistic revolutionaries "total
license to kill." Theirs was the language of the Antichrist, putting "man in
God's place" and mutilating the human soul in the process. This was a truly
demonic project, an assault on God and man.

Scruton saw in ideological revolution and despotism "an incurable nihilism" at work, negating the moral law and the "qualified and partial liberties" in our imperfect but decent societies "which come through the work
of compromise." These revolutions inevitably give rise to the tyranny of
ideological clichés, of murderous euphemisms, where "enemies are demo-
nized in readiness for their liquidation." Jacobinism, the revolutionary terror
that ravaged France between 1792 and 1794, with its own *langue de bois*
and murderous rituals, paved the way for the more consistent totalitarianism of the Communist movement in the twentieth century. The tribunals
of the French Revolution, in its most radical period, provided the imitable
model for revolutionary justice in the twentieth century in the Soviet bloc,

China, Vietnam, Laos, Cambodia, Cuba, Nicaragua, and many half-ideological states in the Middle East and much of modern Africa. In his splendid 1990 essay "Man's Second Disobedience," also to be found in *Philosopher on Dover Beach*, written on the occasion of the bicentennial of the French Revolution, Scruton succinctly sums up the perversities inherent in revolutionary justice:

> Under revolutionary justice you are tried, in the end, not for what you do but for what you are: émigré or kulak, Jew or anti-socialist, enemy of the people or running dog of capitalism—in each case crime is not an action, but a state of being.

In all this Scruton saw "a supreme act of Christian disobedience" where human beings ceased to worship the transcendental God and thus transformed the genuinely sacred into a project of revolutionary negation. The worship of the revolutionary idol annulled the moral law and became a "worship of nothing" but a "potent nothingness, which threatens everything real." Goethe's Mephistopheles, "the spirit that forever negates," readily comes to mind, as Scruton liked to point out. To resist this totalitarian negation, Scruton worked courageously on behalf of the intellectual underground in Czechoslovakia, Poland, and Hungary in the years before 1989. As we have just seen in the previous chapter, Scruton's spiritually luminous novel *Notes from Underground* splendidly captures the atmosphere of those years far better than any account written by political scientists, historians, and journalists. They, in contrast to Scruton, were singularly unprepared to write about the ideological Lie and the reassertion of the human spirit by those who decided, against all odds, to "live in truth."

To resist this perverse assault on the prerogatives of God, Scruton turned his attention to the *imago dei*, the incarnate person, who is indeed an animal, a part of the natural order, but in "whom the light of reason shines, and who looks at us from eyes that tell of freedom." To recover the face of man is to encounter the sacred space which grounds "all respect, and all affection." As Scruton put it with great clarity in "The Philosopher on Dover Beach," "the experience of the sacred is the sudden encounter with freedom; it is the recognition of personality and purposefulness in that which contains no human will." We have thus left Marx, Nietzsche, and

Darwin far behind, and have moved several dramatic steps beyond Kant's moralized replacement for traditional theology. We have recognized the "transcendentals" at the heart of the human experience of the sacred and the human expression of self-conscious freedom.

As a philosopher, Scruton paves the way for the return to religion which is, in his view, "inseparable, in the end, from our sense of holiness" which we discern from the freedom calling out to us from the eyes of another human person. Science, Scruton famously argues, has no power to "forbid the experience of the sacred." When it does so it moves far beyond its competence and imposes on free men and women a stifling materialist ideology that has no room for human persons or moral and civic agency. As Mark Dooley has rightly noted, at the end of this emblematic essay ("The Philosopher on Dover Beach") Scruton provides an eloquent credo which perfectly brings together all his theoretical and practical concerns. Scruton writes:

> [W]ithout the sacred, man lives in a depersonalized world: a world where all is permitted, and where nothing has absolute value. That, I believe, is the principal lesson of modern history, and if we tremble before it, it is because it contains a judgment on us. The hubris which leads us to believe that science has the answer to all our questions, that we are nothing but dying animals and that the meaning of life is mere self-affirmation, or at best the pursuit of some collective, all-embracing and all-too-human goal—this reckless superstition contains already the punishment of those who succumb to it.

This is Scruton's most precise, wise, penetrating, and challenging articulation of the best anti-totalitarian philosophical and political wisdom of our time. Here we confront eloquence at the service of philosophical and spiritual wisdom.

By recovering the person, the animal with freedom and moral responsibility calling out from his eyes, Roger Scruton made a signal contribution to a philosophical, political, and even theological defense and articulation of the sacred and the soul. In his last interview, conducted with the relatively new Hungarian literary-cultural review *Országút* and republished (in English) in the May 2020 issue of the *Hungarian Review*, Scruton explained (in part) why he had returned to the Anglican Church in the later decades of his life: he found, he said, joy and solace in its hymns and Bible stories, "and the experience of Holy Communion force(d) me to be humble and to recognize my faults." To love our inheritance, including our Christian inheritance with all its glories and imperfections, is to recognize the cleansing hope that is repentance and the possibility of a redemption that cannot be complete or final in this world. It is to come to terms with the transcendence at "the edge of things."

Instead of inexpiable conflict and murderous hate—the dead-end offered by loveless and ungrateful ideologues—one begins to discern the path of forgiveness. Earlier in the same interview, however, Scruton asked why leftists, hard and soft, "find forgiveness so difficult?" As we see all around us, they succumb ever so quickly to the temptation to annul, cancel, or eliminate their real and imagined enemies. This, Scruton suggests, "surely" is "the great question of 20th-century politics." As a new cultural revolution strikes at the very heart of our cultural, political, and civilizational inheritance, that prescient and challenging question serves as one more reminder of the philosophical and human greatness of Roger Scruton. May we take inspiration from his wisdom and his thoughtful and vigorous defense of civilization, the sacred, and the soul.

## Sources and Suggested Readings

The core of this chapter is based on a close critical reading of two essays, "The Philosopher on Dover Beach," and "Man's Second Disobedience" in Roger Scruton's *Philosopher on Dover Beach*, published by St. Augustine's in 1990 and 1998, respectively. I am also indebted to Mark Dooley's lucid and inviting reading of Scruton's philosophizing, and of the aforementioned two essays, in *Roger Scruton: The Philosopher on Dover Beach* (Continuum, 2009).

Scruton's *Beauty: A Very Short Introduction* (Oxford, 2009) is an impressive response to those who see the aesthetic realm as a realm of pure subjectivity. There is, Scruton insists, such a thing as right appreciation of beautiful things.

# Chapter 8
# INVENTING THE AUTHORITY OF A MODERN SELF

As we have shown in chapter 2, Pierre Manent has spent four decades chronicling the development of modern self-consciousness, including the flight from human nature and "the moral contents of life" that define modern self-understanding in its most radical forms. Manent's work thus combines penetrating analyses of great works of political, philosophical, and religious reflection with judicious independent thought. In both, he illumines the interpenetration of politics and the things of the soul. That dialectical melding of politics and soul permanently defines the human condition, even in the most remote times and climes. It is one profound reason we can speak of a human nature shared by thinking and acting human beings as such.

Manent continued that work with learning and grace in his 2014 *Montaigne: Life without Law* (2020 for the English-language edition).[1] Montaigne (1533–92) is much more than a literary figure for Manent. His Montaigne is first and foremost a philosopher and a moral reformer, even a founder of one vitally important strain of modern self-understanding. In this new form of consciousness, human beings take their bearing neither from great models of heroism or sanctity or wisdom, nor from natural and divine law. Rather, Montaigne asks his readers to eschew self-transcending admiration for others, no matter how exemplary great souls may seem to

---

1   *Montaigne: Life without Law*, by Pierre Manent, translated by Paul Seaton (Notre Dame, IN: University of Notre Dame Press, 2020). The original French edition, *Montaigne: La vie sans loi* came out from Flammarion in 2014. A paperback edition came out in French in January 2021. All quotations and references are cited parenthetically in the text as *MLWL* followed by the appropriate page number or numbers.

be. He wishes those who follow him to reject the path of repentance for sins, and to bow before the demands and requirements of one's unique self, what he calls one's "master-form" (*MLWL*, 61). A reading of his *Essays*, written, published, and revised between 1570 and 1592, demonstrate that he genuinely admired Socrates and the Roman hero Cato. But Montaigne rather shockingly claims to have learned nothing fundamental from them, and he has no interest whatsoever in imitating their greatness, or that of any other. Nonetheless, there is something enticing about Montaigne's turn to the authority of the self in place of the classical Christian demand to put order in one's soul in light of the requirements of the Good itself. Many readers over the centuries have succumbed to Montaigne's considerable charms and deeply impressive artistry, and sometimes quite uncritically at that.

Manent includes Montaigne among the great modern founders and reformers, rivaled only by his immediate predecessors Machiavelli and Jean Calvin. A paradigmatic modern founder and reformer such as Calvin tried "to liberate the truth from the human intermediaries" (*MLWL*, 3) that he believed stood in the way of a direct relation between God and each individual soul. But once one rejects "ecclesiastical mediation," Manent asks, why stop with the authority of scripture itself? All distances, all superintending moral authorities, become suspect under the new dispensation. Calvin would be appalled by modern appeals to groundless human autonomy and to the "self" in place of the authoritative Word of God. In addition, Calvin says little to those "disinclined to piety" (*MLWL*, 7), surely the majority of human beings caught up in the pressing demands of ordinary life. In his turn, the greatest political reformer-founder of modernity, Machiavelli, says little or nothing to the human being "without ambition" (*MLWL*, 7). Montaigne limns a third modernist path, one that defers neither to the Word of God, nor to the temptation of a glory-seeking republican political life. His path is as far from piety as it is from amoral Machiavellian political self-assertion. He limns the path of private, idiosyncratic, and this-worldly contentment.

Manent ably establishes that Montaigne does indeed have an authority to which he defers. That authority "is life itself in its ordinary tenor, in the variation of humors and the irregularity of its accidents" (*MLWL*, 7). Life, however, in Manent's formulation "needs to be brought to life and, if I can put it in this way, installed in a light that causes its fullness to appear, while preserving its imperfection" (*MLWL*, 7). This is Montaigne's great revolutionary aim. Manent's brilliant book throws light on a paradox of the highest order in connection with that aim. Montaigne's account of the new model man appears eminently human and humane, but in truth it is unthinkable and unlivable. This is because "life without law" (*MLWL*, 179) strips humanity of true self-knowledge and the accompanying capacity for reasonable moral and political choice, and also moral reformation. Moreover, as Blaise Pascal complained in his *Pensées*, published in 1670, eight years after his own death, Montaigne talked far too much about himself, the only authority he treated as genuinely authoritative. In the end, there is something deeply solipsistic and even unnaturally antinomian about Montaigne's new model of the moral life. That Pascal saw with emblematic clarity.

Pascal admired Montaigne's *Essays* and constantly cited or appropriated passages from them, even as Montaigne's replacement of the soul with the self genuinely horrified him. Following Pascal, Manent notes Montaigne's radical rejection—in the great essay "On Repentance" from Book III of the *Essays* —of repentance and of the need to prepare oneself for a truly Christian death. Accepting one's "master-form," and rejecting repentance as of dubious "sincerity," leads Montaigne to the conclusion that neither he, nor any other man or woman, can really do better. We are, in effect, destined to navigate within the parameters of our own unique "master-form." Reform, repentance, or conversion are not sincere or authentic human possibilities. Quietly but firmly, Montaigne ends "by expelling from human life every rule, every principle, capable of guiding it, every criterion of the better" (*MLWL*, 55).

But in an important respect, Manent does not believe Montaigne's claim. Montaigne calls himself "an unpremeditated and accidental philosopher" since his self, even though it points toward "so many philosophical examples and reasons" (*MLWL*, 55), remains closed to all wisdom outside itself. Manent asks, can it truly be the case that Montaigne "was never internally divided by a law that he was to obey nor guided by a teaching he was convinced he ought to follow, nor even moved by a model to which he ought to conform?" Was Montaigne miraculously free from the drama of good and evil that is constitutive of every human soul? Was he so self-contained that "he simply developed according to nature, which is to say *his* nature" (*MLWL*, 55) and not human nature *tout court*? Montaigne's account of the self, his self, is, strictly speaking, unbelievable. But it has become the default position of those who affirm the primacy of the self, freed from any connection to ends and purposes outside the immediate self that point to a life well lived in accordance with goodness and truth. Through this lens, Montaigne's alluring humanism seems far less humane than it does at an initial glance.

He himself gives reasons for this sort of hesitation. In "The Apology for Raymond Sebond," the longest of his essays by far, Montaigne tells us he sees no essential differences between human beings and animals, and sometimes judges animals to be quite superior in judgment and character (*MLWL*, 189–90). We are surely in uncharted territory.

Pascal was appalled by Montaigne's advice to his readers that they approach death "without fear or repentance." He thought Montaigne's completely pagan views on death and repentance were "inexcusable." Nor was this simply offered from the point of view of faith. Montaigne recommended "a death of cowardly ease," where one diverts oneself from the most fundamental and consequential questions of human existence. As a Christian, however, Pascal offered an alternative of a humiliation that led, paradoxically, to elevation and ultimate redemption. As Manent argues in *Pascal et la proposition chrétienne* (published by Grasset in October 2022), human beings are obliged to think very seriously (and directly) about the reality, and imminence, of death. We must live honorably, nobly, even when our self-preservation is at stake (here Pascal is at one with the spirit of classical political philosophy). But Stoics such as Epictetus delude themselves when they deny that "pain and death are not evils," to cite Pascal's own words. Montaigne deludes himself when he encourages human beings to evade death in a spirit of "cowardice" and "softness" (*MLWL*, 28–30), as Pascal puts it. To fear death, to confront one's mortality openly and self-consciously is to put mortal man in touch with the "greatness and misery" that defines the condition of human beings in a "fallen" or imperfect world. To be indifferent to the palpable reality of death is to close oneself off to the larger purpose of life and to the hope that arguably lies on the other side of death.

To be sure, Montaigne is not a vulgar relativist: he still acknowledges the high (Socrates and Cato) and the low (men, quite numerous in his time, who administered torture and cruelty). He admirably despised fanaticism and religious wars. But in the end, "it is the master-form of each, which is what it is, but which necessarily constitutes the only base of operations for a human conduct that knows itself" (*MLWL*, 61). Montaigne defends a humility of sorts, but one completely upended from a Christian frame or horizon (*MLWL*, 63). In these and other ways, Manent conclusively demonstrates that Montaigne decisively breaks with both the Christian and Socratic perspectives, the bedrock of what thinkers in the Western tradition call "sapiential" wisdom.

All three perspectives, the classical-Socratic one, the Christian one, and Montaigne's new conception of the self, aim for self-knowledge. But Manent incisively shows that true self-knowledge must be arrived at indirectly and cannot be willed into being (*MLWL*, 88). A precondition of self-knowledge and spiritual growth for the classics and Christians alike is "the putting in order of the soul," a process that requires conversion or *metanoia*. The faculties and dispositions of the soul must be ordered by turning to the light of truth and obeying the requirements of non-subjectivist conscience. Self-knowledge is therefore unthinkable without an *effort* to *perfect* the soul (*MLWL*, 88). To take one's bearings from one's "self" is to finally take one's bearings from nothing substantial or enduring.

But Montaigne's substitute for the soul, the self or master-form, makes no such demands to perfect or even improve the soul. To reject the soul and the arduous task of ordering it and elevating it is, willy-nilly, to be content with the self as it is. Vulgarized and popularized, Montaigne's account of the self has predictably produced men and women who lack Montaigne's remarkable classical learning and his capacity to admire (if not imitate) Socrates and Cato. It leads inexorably to what C. S. Lewis called "the poison of subjectivism," where the soul is severed from conscience rightly understood and liberated from that *eros* of the mind that allows us to discover the freedom and grace that accompany true self-transcendence. Montaigne entombed this precious heritage in the serpentine labyrinth of his *Essays* without the vast majority of readers noticing. But Pascal noticed and Manent powerfully renews his concerns.

Manent has three additional insights about Montaigne's modern moral reformation that shed important light on our situation. In a penetrating analysis of the famous essay "On Cannibals," Manent shows how

Montaigne pioneered the cultural relativism in contemporary anthropology and ethnology that asserts, in effect, that "all 'cultures' are equally rational" and that "all 'cultures' are equally irrational" (*MLWL*, 142–43). The latter point is of decisive significance.

Montaigne was not wrong to argue that civilized people, especially during the wars of religion, committed numerous barbaric acts. Here Montaigne's aversion to fanaticism and what Machiavelli before him called "pious cruelty" (*Prince*, chapter 21) is quite admirable. But by effacing any difference between civilization and barbarism, Montaigne has left us with an infinite diversity of customs, none in principle better than the other. He thus undercuts the grounds of his own moral judgment. Montaigne's sophisticated cultural relativism inevitably gave rise over time to a vulgar cultural relativism, one we are still living with. Such an approach, Manent rightly observes, is simply and "entirely incapable of guiding action" (*MLWL*, 143). It necessarily disarms civilization in any encounter with barbarism, even if the learned and humane Montaigne was no barbarian.

Secondly, as the translator of the book Paul Seaton notes in an excellent foreword that accompanies his translation, Montaigne opts for a "self-sufficient private life that, by writing, creates the 'public' that is invited to become privy to his 'candor and human wisdom.'" Montaigne is the first and principal creator of the modern "republic of letters."

Lastly, Manent exposes the fully radical, even revolutionary, character of Montaigne's moral reformation. Montaigne is much more than an "accidental" philosopher: he aims at nothing less than putting forward a "new law" for Western civilization, where the law is commanded "not to command." The genial Montaigne is the principal architect of the subversive "hypothesis that human beings can lead a life without law" (*MLWL*, 178), natural or otherwise. Over several centuries, Montaigne's valorization of the self gave way to a "dictatorship of relativism" that commands us in the name of autonomy and authenticity to disregard all law, all command, all moral authority. Rights thus become increasingly disconnected from any appreciation of the ends and purposes that are inherent in moral judgment and prudential choice. Would the civilized Montaigne applaud what he has wrought? I have my doubts, even if it is hard to conjecture.

In a remarkable book that we have already introduced entitled *Natural Law and Human Rights: Toward a Recovery of Practical Reason*, also published in English in 2020 by the University of Notre Dame Press, Manent responds to Montaigne's challenge. Here Manent persuasively defends the enduring relevance of the old cardinal virtues—courage, justice, prudence, and moderation—and of a conception of non-arbitrary conscience that can provide practical reason with rich moral content. And he argues that the principal motives of human action—the pleasant, the useful, and the noble, properly conjugated—define the criteria for moral judgment and political action, in every time and place. In these two recently translated books, Manent continues his impressive political and philosophical efforts to reconnect human liberty with natural law, practical reason, and the moral contents of life. This is moral and political philosophy of a very high order, and of great and enduring relevance. The French political philosopher reminds us that the self is not the soul, and that liberty is nothing more than a void without "law" to inform and guide it.

# Chapter 9
# THE CONSCIENCE OF THE CONSERVATIVE: READING *AGAINST THE TIDE*

In his lucid and succinct "Preface" to *Against the Tide*, an authoritative and wide-ranging collection of Roger Scruton's journalism, columns, review essays, and occasional diary entries written between 1971 and 2019, Scruton's literary executor, the Irish philosopher and journalist Mark Dooley, suggestively compares Scruton to the German philosopher Hegel. Scruton, like Hegel at his best, saw the intellectual life as "a spiritual endeavor to synthesize art, music, religion, politics, and philosophy" (Dooley in *ATT*, x).

Of course, Scruton did not share Hegel's historicist confidence in the possibility of human beings reaching an "end to History" where all "contradictions" are in principle resolved, or attaining a Wisdom that is at once final and definitive. That sort of Hegelianism was wholly alien to Scruton who remained faithful to the Platonic view that "care of the soul" was inseparable from care of the polis, two vital imperatives that would confront human beings as long as a distinctively human condition endured. But the aspiration to do justice to the full range of human experience and the highest forms of human understanding and creativity gave an unmistakably Hegelian tinge to Scruton's own efforts at practical philosophizing. Scruton not only read the morning newspapers, to allude to a quintessentially Hegelian motif, but he wrote for them with clarity, insight, and eloquence. As Dooley observes, Roger Scruton was a gifted writer before anything else. At first glance, Scruton's truly elegant writing seems effortless. But it was in fact the product of considerable craft, a sustained effort on his part to become one of the great men of letters of his time. To reduce him to the level of conservative polemicist or controversialist is to commit a serious injustice.

Scruton, was, nonetheless, a conservative of a particularly urbane kind. The writings expertly collected in *Against the Tide* go a long way toward illuminating Scruton's humane and dignified conservatism. The reader relives the creation in 1982 of *The Salisbury Review*, Britain's first unabashedly conservative intellectual review (*ATT*, 3–7). The review's contributors included such eminent writers and thinkers as Peter Bauer, A. L. Rowse, Václav Havel, P. D. James, and Scruton himself. It eventually found itself a devoted readership in samizdat in communist East-Central Europe where Scruton had developed close ties with the intellectual underground.

At home, Scruton and *The Salisbury Review* were subjected to furious criticism in academic circles and in the left-liberal press. Every effort was made to "cancel" the humane and cultivated Scruton for "crimes" that included intelligent anti-communism, moral clarity about what is entailed in limitless immigration and unguarded borders, a thoughtful defense of British sovereignty and the nation-state, and the firmest opposition to "the culture of repudiation" in all its forms. Readers of *Against the Tide* will quickly come to appreciate that the war on the West is longstanding and that political correctness has been ensconced in the commanding heights of journalism and educational and cultural institutions for five decades or more. Scruton had been fighting the good fight decades before many *soi-disant* conservatives even noticed there was a battle. They were so preoccupied with the alterations of the business cycle and the political pendulum that they failed to truly appreciate that the West was losing its soul. There is a profound lesson in all of that.

Scruton's urbane conservatism had no time of day for what he called in a 1994 piece ("The Conservative Conscience") "trivializing materialists and sarcastic cynics" (*ATT*, 33) who increasingly dominated media and cultural life in Britain and elsewhere and who showed open contempt for traditional affirmations. He opposed totalitarian collectivism and unremitting efforts to nationalize and centralize political and economic life. But as he argued in a 2018 essay on "What Donald Trump Doesn't Get About Conservatism," the best conservative thinkers "on the whole praised the free market, but they do not think that market values are the only values out there." Conservatism above all cherishes "What cannot be bought and sold: things like love, loyalty, art, and knowledge, which are not means to an end but ends in themselves" (*ATT*, 54–56, especially 56). Trump deserved credit

RECOVERING POLITICS, CIVILIZATION, AND THE SOUL

for standing up to political correctness and fighting the tyrannical leftist mob. But like that mob, he was a product of social media and "cultural decline." And his vulgarity had nothing to do with the broader conservative intellectual tradition that Scruton so energetically and thoughtfully defended. It is hard to dispute these tough-minded claims.

In contrast, as a 2013 column from the *London Times* makes clear, Scruton genuinely admired Margaret Thatcher's character and achievement. But her greatest legacy was, in his view, not the market-minded reform of British political economy, as necessary and desirable as it undoubtedly was, but her placing "the nation and national interest at the center of politics" (*ATT*, 48) once again. Readers of a certain age will remember her great September 20, 1988, speech at Bruges where she took to task the very idea of a Europe-Behemoth. She was the first British statesman in two generations to defend national sovereignty as the crucial precondition of self-government and democracy rightly understood.

Only territorial democracy, as Scruton wrote elsewhere, allowed free men and women to remain accountable to each other. National identification allows people of different religions, tribes, and ethnicity, strangers in other respects, to live under a shared system of law. And he sympathized with the desire of the peoples of East-Central Europe to hold on to their national patrimonies after the brutal and bitter experience of a half-century of ideological despotism. Scruton sympathized with the concerns of Hungarians, Poles, and Czechs that their tutelage to a cruel ideological despotism was being replaced by a new empire of centralized regulation, radical secularism, moral relativism, and diminished national sovereignty in the form of an ever more capricious European Union. Thatcher saw much of this coming while her contemporaries thought only in terms of material prosperity and all-democratic bliss.

In my judgment, the most profound aspect of *Against the Tide* is its ample and persuasive (non- or extra-theological) defense of the soul in Part IV of the book ("Intimations of Infinity," *ATT*, 89–112), themes we have already addressed in chapter seven. In this section, Scruton argues vigorously against theoretical and practical materialism and every form of scientistic reductionism. He took the "life-world," rooted in common sense and ordinary experience, with the true seriousness it deserves. When we respond to another human being, we are responding to an ensouled person and not just a conglomeration of matter-in-motion. "Nothing-buttery" (*ATT*, 111) as the English philosopher Mary Midgley so suggestively called it, can only see flesh and physical laws in a world of freely acting, thinking, and judging persons. But modern reductionists, and the evermore censorious "new atheists," see in the human being only instinct and animality, in law "nothing but" power (a view theorized, or rather propagandized, by Michel Foucault and the full range of postmodernists), in sexual love "nothing but" the "procreative urge," and in the *Mona Lisa* "nothing but" the "spread of pigments on a canvas" (*ATT*, 111). Nothing-buttery simply explains away the human person, lived experience, and truth as well as love and beauty. It dogmatically eviscerates what is most dear to human beings and that is at the center of our personal experience. And how are philosophy or science even possible if the human person as philosopher or scientist doesn't even exist? How do true freedom, the search for truth, and the mutual accountability at the heart of interpersonal relations make sense in a world where predetermined causal relations and scientistic reduction reign supreme? Nothing-buttery assumes a world without human beings.

More boldly, Scruton rejects "nothing-buttery" in the big things as well as the small. If sex, pictures, and people are not reducible to something other than themselves, why should that be the case "when dealing with the world as a whole"? The world is no more reducible to the "order of nature as physics describes it" than Da Vinci's *Mona Lisa* is reducible to "nothing but a smear of pigments." Philosophy, rightly understood, and religion at its most thoughtful, are united in defending the human soul and what Scruton elsewhere calls (in a 2015 book by that name) "the soul of the world." Scruton tellingly adds in a 2014 essay on the human hunger for the sacred, that communism, as Scruton experienced it during his numerous clandestine visits behind the Iron Curtain between 1979 and 1989, provided the *reductio ad absurdum* of a human world reduced to a crudely "scientific worldview" that effaced liberty, human dignity, true philosophy and the sacred as revealed and reflected in the Christian religion. This ultimate form of ideological "nothing-buttery" led to cruel despotism, a systematic assault on the human soul, and a social condition marked by "absolute enmity and distrust." The best of the dissidents in the communist East fought for truth, liberty, beauty, and a soul unmenaced by ideological lies. They did not just fight for "rights," "higher living standards," and "freedom of movement" as the dominant narrative states. That was the path of the dreaded Professor Gunther, and not the dissident world at its most noble and sublime.

Their noble partisanship on behalf of national memory, the sacred and the soul, and liberty tied to conscience and responsibility, is a gift for the ages, a moral witness worth treasuring. But as Scruton remarked in a 2009 column published in *The Times* of London to commemorate the "Velvet Revolution" of 1989, the long-suffering countries of East-Central Europe "bear no resemblance to the liberated nations that were dreamed of in the catacombs. For, when the stones were lifted and the air of freedom blew across the underground altars, the flame that has been kept alive on them was instantly blown out" (*ATT*, 22), blown out by untrammeled freedom, and a desire to unthinkingly replicate the materialist cornucopia that is the West. Perhaps this is why Scruton wrote and published his great anti-totalitarian novel *Notes from Underground*, which we have already examined at great length. Set in the Czech lands that he had come to love, it memorializes (and keeps alive) the loving spirit of conscience and conscientiousness, of deep appreciation of the soul and the sacred, that found true expression in the catacombs. In the catacombs, there was no place for "nothing-buttery." *Against the Tide* and *Notes from Underground* pursue the same themes, and defend the same insights, in both prose and poetry, one as eloquent as the other.

The ending of Scruton's tale is by now well known. We have already told the essentials of the story in chapter one. Under assault from a mendacious young interviewer at the leftist *New Statesman*, who fabricated quotations to justify Scruton's cancellation as an anti-Semite, Islamophobe, and hater of all sorts, Scruton was summarily fired as the head of a government commission charged with addressing the "uglification" of British architecture and town planning. Only after the true tapes of the notorious interview were recovered by the intrepid journalist Douglas Murray, was Scruton vindicated and restored to his position. Torn down by a vindicative leftist mob abated by cowardly Tories, Scruton, now dying of cancer, was publicly honored with the highest national medals by his old friends and admirers in Poland, the Czech Republic, and Hungary. And decent and truth-loving souls, friends and strangers alike, came to his defense from all over the world. Scruton found solace in such displays of friendship and in the ultimately joyful account in the Gospel of Christ's death and resurrection (see his deeply moving 2019 column "After My Own Dark Night"). In his final diary entry in the book, dated December 2019, Scruton notes with quiet, moving eloquence:

> Falling to the bottom in my own country, I have been raised to the top elsewhere, and looking back over the sequence of events I can only be glad that I have lived long enough to see this happen. Coming close to death you begin to know what life means, and what it means is gratitude *(ATT,* 231).

To hear these moving words is to hear Roger Scruton from the depth of his heart, mind, and soul. What a noble legacy he has left us. Instead of *fiat* and self-assertion, he restores gratitude and grace to their central place in the order of things. Like Pierre Manent in a different but largely complementary way, he opens his heart and mind to the evidence that the Good is not unsupported, that truth and moral value are rooted in the very "soul of the world." That affirmation not only restores a common world to us but is powerfully and profoundly "against the tide."

## Sources and Suggested Readings

All quotations and citations to *Against the Tide: The Best of Roger Scruton's Columns, Commentaries, and Criticism,* edited by Mark Dooley (Bloomsbury Continuum, 2022), are cited parenthetically in the text as *ATT* followed by the appropriate page or page numbers.

# Chapter 10

# WITH REASON ATTENTIVE TO GRACE: PIERRE MANENT'S CORRECTION OF LIBERALISM AND CHRISTIAN UTOPIANISM

For forty-five years or more, Pierre Manent has explored the tensions inherent in "the theological-political problem" as they manifest themselves in late modernity and in the human condition or situation more broadly. As we have seen, Manent is a convert to Catholicism (he was raised in a Communist family), a student of Raymond Aron, and from there on an anti-totalitarian of the first order. Manent is also a political philosopher who unequivocally upholds the truth of the "Christian proposition," as he calls it. Yet, as I shall show, he does not take his political bearings from theological categories or from revelation per se. He is first and foremost a political philosopher who takes his bearings from reason, from the natural order of things, while being fully attentive to the workings of grace and conscience on the souls and free will of human beings. Manent rejects political theology, political deductions from explicitly theoretical categories or dogmas, whether put forward by a Catholic decisionist such as Carl Schmitt, the demi-Marxist liberation theologians, the quasi-theocratic integralists, or the proponents of "Radical Orthodoxy" such as John Milbank, with their imprudent disdain for everything connected to the liberal or bourgeois order.

Let us return to Manent's own intellectual itinerary already explored in chapter two. His conversion owes much to Louis Jugnet, a teacher of Manent's at a lycée in Toulouse and a Thomist of "strict observance," who introduced him to the ample and salutary role of "right reason" in Thomistic philosophical and theological reflection.[1] Manent remains

---

1    See Pierre Manent, *Seeing Things Politically: Interviews with Benedicte Delorme-*

indebted to the Thomistic "analysis of virtues, of prudence and justice, [its] analysis of action, of deliberation and of rational choice"[2]—and, one might add, to its effort to find a rightful place for the prudence and free will of human beings in God's providential design. But as Manent remarks in his autobiographical book of conversations, *Seeing Things Politically*, the Thomist appropriation of Aristotelian wisdom is "almost completely detached from [Aristotle's] political context and . . . political concerns." This "noble intellectual tradition" has largely "moralized and depoliticized Aristotle." It tends to look "at political experience 'from above'"[3] and to read Aristotle's *Ethics* in complete abstraction from his *Politics*. For all its ethical and metaphysical insights, it is thus of limited validity to the political philosopher, Christian or otherwise. But as we shall see, a more political or prudent Thomism will play a crucial role in Manent's subsequent rearticulation of the relationship between practical reason and the Christian proposition.

## Manent's "Triangle" Revisited: Politics, Philosophy, and Religion

But Manent remains at best a demi-Thomist, since he is preoccupied, in his own self-description, with the "triangle" of "politics, philosophy, and religion" in a way that refuses "complete devotion," at least complete intellectual devotion, to any of these competing human attitudes or orientations. In a profound existential sense, the religious man cannot be a philosopher "in the full sense" even if he can "employ philosophical tools very competently," since he "has answered the Call that precedes all questions." A magnanimous statesman such as Churchill is "too busy with 'human things'" to truly be a philosopher or religious man, while a certain kind of "philosopher"—say, Socrates or Leo Strauss (to mention a great figure closer to home who has been a significant influence on Manent)—turns away from

*Montini*, trans. Ralph C. Hancock, with introduction by Daniel J. Mahoney (South Bend, IN: St. Augustine's Press, 2015), 20–22.

2 Ibid., 47.

3 These quotations about the Thomistic appropriation of Aristotelian wisdom can be found in ibid., 47.

human things "not to attend to the Father's" concerns, "but in order to pursue endless questioning."

Manent, in contrast, has committed himself to what he calls "a fragile equilibrium, or rather a productive disequilibrium," with the intent of "treating each of the three equally seriously."[4] That does not mean that Manent is not a believer: he most emphatically is a Christian of conviction. But he is one who refuses to let either philosophical reflection or religious devotion get in the way of allowing the "simply human perspective" from receiving its full due, something he believes both political theology, and a certain rarified form of piety, fails to do. He thus starts his inquiries with a precise and demanding phenomenology of the human city and the human soul. In Manent's view, Christianity and political philosophy must both begin by maintaining scrupulous fidelity to the "real" as it first comes to sight in human experience. Nature necessarily precedes grace in the human experience of things. To begin with grace, or the "sacred," or the transcendent, is to risk obscuring the real.

## Péguy and the Imperative Not to Despise the Natural Order

Here, Manent takes his bearings from Charles Péguy's commentary on Pierre Corneille's *Polyeucte*, a great spiritual and political drama set in third-century Armenia. Manent, following Péguy, sees Corneille (a classic seventeenth-century French dramatist and the closest to a French equivalent of Shakespeare) as an exemplary Christian author who "does not pull down the world in order to elevate religion." Polyeucte is "not satisfied with having the truth for himself" despite the fact that he has just converted to Christianity. He has admirably opened himself up to divine grace but still wants "to be the equal of Severus, the Roman knight," equal to him on the plane (and perhaps even surpassing him on that plane) "in exercising human virtues," particularly "those of human honor and human generosity."[5] Polyeucte admirably wishes to partake in both the order of nature and the order of grace, and he does not wish to bypass the first to arrive more quickly at the second.

4   All the quotations in this paragraph are from ibid. 59–60.
5   Ibid., 61–62.

Manent, following two major Catholic authors, Corneille and Péguy, is committed to not "pull[ing] down the world in order to elevate religion." The natural virtues, the cardinal virtues, must be taken on their own terms without the misbegotten view that the order of grace leaves the pagan virtues or human honor behind, minimizing them or even depreciating them in the process of spiritual ascent. Humble deference to the beneficence and providence of God our Father and Friend need not leave the Roman virtues of courage and prudence behind. Humility and magnanimity, a certain pride in our own natural and civic resources, are the two wellsprings of the human soul and of a Western civilization worthy of the name. In *Seeing Things Politically*, Manent even endorses Péguy's rather "brutal warning" to the "devout party" not "to believe that they are people of grace because they lack the strength to be of nature."[6] As we shall see, this understanding of the integrity of the "natural order of things" has much to do with Pierre Manent's rejection of "political theology" as a choice-worthy or viable enterprise. Political theology is not phenomenological enough—it does not begin in the beginning. In contrast, the political philosophy Manent advocates and practices, open to biblical wisdom, is much better prepared to do justice to the competing and tension-ridden—yet ultimately complementary—demands of nature and grace, truth and liberty, greatness of soul and humble deference to the Most High. Manent's is a project of *mediation*, attentive to the capacious balancing of the genuine goods of life, the city, and the soul, and of reason and the Christian proposition more broadly. Contra Leo Strauss, such mediation should not be confused with a facile and misplaced synthesis of all good things.

## The Christian, the Cardinal Virtues, and Political Freedom

A due respect for the cardinal virtues—courage, temperance, justice, and prudence—must precede every effort to sanctify the world. As Manent put it at his farewell address at the École des Hautes Études on June 13, 2014, "Action stood before Pericles, it stood before Paul of Tarsus, and it stands before us. The question is to know how we can put the city's reasons to work, and thus what is our courage, what is our moderation, what is our

6    All quotations in this paragraph are from ibid., 61–62.

justice, what is our prudence."[7] With C. S. Lewis and Rémi Brague, Manent does not believe that there is a distinctive *Christian* ethics or politics per se. Yet the Christian Gospel introduces "the commandment to love our enemies," and we are obliged to use the arts of intelligence to come to terms with that most difficult and challenging demand on our souls.[8] This is the sempiternal structure of moral-political reality, and no historical process or ideological constructions can free us from our natural and supernatural responsibilities and obligations.

Manent believes that Christianity has a real, if complicated and somewhat tenuous, relationship to political freedom. The Christian tradition is anti-totalitarian to the core, since one cannot render to Caesar what is not his due (Matthew 22:21). And in the Acts of the Apostles (5:9), Peter adds more forcefully that one must "obey God rather than man." The Gospels, and the larger biblical tradition, categorically and rightly reject every effort at human self-deification. Yet the Catholic Church, in particular, was often too suspicious of the pride and self-assertion associated with liberal and national movements. Republican liberty at its best produces "virile citizens," and "virile virtues," as both Aristotle and Tocqueville remind us. In contrast, the Catholic Church often preferred the relatively quiescent subjects of clerical and authoritarian regimes (one is reminded of Dolfuss's Austria and Salazar's Portugal in the first half of the twentieth century) to the "pride and ambition" of republican citizens who had "confidence in their own powers."[9] There are grave risks in that direction, too.

## Free Will, Conscience, and Reflective Choice

Yet free will, reflective choice (as Aristotle called it), and moral responsibility, all crucial to a regime of liberty, vitally depend on conscience, "the interior space . . . that was discovered or invented by Christianity." This internal and invisible tribunal allows us to judge our own and others' actions as God himself would judge them. Manent strikingly observes that

7    See the appendix entitled "Knowledge and Politics," in *Seeing Things Politically*, 197–211, and see 207 for the quotation.
8    Ibid., 207.
9    Manent, *Seeing Things Politically*, 170.

"the Greeks had a marvelous understanding of the movements of our soul, but they knew nothing of conscience." That was a defect of real importance. Their profound sense of the visibility of the virtuous soul left them with no ears "for the voice of conscience," which is "something one listens to."[10] Christianity is in important respects a transpolitical religion that nonetheless opened up "the invisible domain" of conscience in ways that are crucial to human self-understanding and to the exercise of moral and political agency. It thus had a powerful, if indirect, relevance to political life.

Yet the early modern philosophers—Machiavelli, Hobbes, Bayle, and Spinoza, among them—would expel from their emerging science of politics both Aristotelian prudence or reflective choice and the free will and conscience that "emerged in the context of Christianity."[11] Machiavelli, in particular, put forward a new and radically paradoxical view of human freedom that was tethered to necessity and that aimed to displace nonsubjectivist conscience and practical reason from human and political life. But for Manent, Aristotle and Christianity, reflective choice and free will and conscience, stand or fall together. They are the indispensable ground of practical life, practical reason, and moral and political agency. Manent draws on the full resources of classical and Christian wisdom to defend "liberty under law." In the early modern period it was confronted with two profound challenges, both the "Christian liberty" of Martin Luther, contemptuous as it was of natural law and the requirements of conscience, as well as the Machiavellian endorsement of infinite moral flexibility in the soul of the prince (see chapter 18 of *The Prince*) and of the reckless and audacious "conquest of *fortuna*" that informs the whole of theoretical modernity (see chapter 25 of *The Prince*).[12]

In his latest book, *Natural Law and Human Rights: Toward the Recovery of Practical Reason*, which I have been drawing upon, Manent argues that

---

10 All quotations in this paragraph are from *Seeing Things Politically*, 168–70.

11 On the modern philosophical assault on free will, see Manent, *Natural Rights and Human Rights: Toward a Recovery of Practical Reason*, trans. Ralph C. Hancock, with foreword by Daniel J. Mahoney (Notre Dame, IN: University of Notre Dame Press, 2020), 87–89.

12 See Manent's discussion of Machiavelli's and Luther's distinct but complementary assaults on natural law and conscience in Manent, *Natural Law and Human Rights*, 24–41.

"the notion of conscience," traditionally understood, "supports and complements the Aristotelian analysis of practical life and of reflective choice so well that the two elements prove to be inseparable."[13] Once nonsubjectivist conscience is dismissed as a fiction or fairy tale, practical philosophy and the arts of prudence become well-nigh impossible. Human beings lose the tools to understand themselves and the human world. We moderns and late moderns literally become inarticulate. In the process, our very capacity for reasonable judgment, prudent choice, and moral responsibility erodes and loses its intelligibility. Choice is severed from reasonable ends, and any meaningful criteria to guide thought or action.

## A Return to Commanding Reason and Reflective Choice

Political theology cannot lead us out of our desperate straits. Rather, what is first needed is a return to common sense and common experience, to a clear-eyed appreciation of the "natural order of things" and of the goods and motives that inform the human soul and that give rise to action guided by free will and conscience. Manent freely acknowledges that most of the philosophers and political philosophers who first inspired and articulated the liberal project sincerely wished "to liberate humanity from the shackles [and superstitions] that held them back and constrained them." But the almost immediate turn of these thinkers to scientistic reductionism, and their accompanying rejection of free will and conscience, made modern men and women less and less "capable of the practical operation that the Greeks thus called reflective choice and that the Christians called free action." With the best of intentions, perhaps, the "fathers of liberalism" created an individual whose decisions were increasingly determined in a mechanistic or quasi-mechanistic way. Despite the bluster that accompanies the modern affirmation of human autonomy, the modern individual is not seen, and does not understand himself, "as a truly free agent."[14] His autonomy is largely illusory. He thus oscillates between inhuman appeals to "necessity," and "determinism," and radical affirmation of a pure or groundless freedom.

What is needed is a classical and Christian reaffirmation of "commanding

13   Ibid., 133 n21.
14   Ibid., 88.

reason,"[15] wherein human persons, guided by reflective choice, conscience, and free will are neither playthings of necessity nor existentialists guided by nothing other than the groundless and contentless affirmation of the will, puffed-up "commitment" without rhyme or reason. The view of the agent that Manent defends avoids what Leo Strauss once so suggestively called (in the final chapter of *Natural Right and History*) the twin extremes (and errors) of the doctrinaire and the existentialist: all-encompassing necessity, on the one hand, and freedom divorced from commanding reason and the goods, ends, purposes, and finalities inherent in the exercise of human freedom, on the other.

## Beyond Autonomy and Heteronomy

Freedom, Manent argues, can never be "the ultimate or main goal to a human being endowed with free will, an agent capable of reflective choice." As already noted, the free agent aims at what commanding reason, high moral and political prudence "commands him," that is "right action, whose declensions are courage, justice, prudence, and temperance—in brief action that takes on its form and color according to the catalogue of the virtues." Commanding reason, "far from injuring action, gives it its rule and meaning."[16] In Manent's view, the "grammar" of moral and political agency transcends the false distinction between "autonomy" and heteronomy" beloved by modern moral philosophers. Liberty is unthinkable, and it cannot give rise to a coherent practical operation, to meaningful and reasonable choice, without the humane but commanding law that gives it substance, content, and direction.

But "commanding reason" also depends crucially on human freedom. In an appendix to *Natural Law and Human Rights* called "Recovering Law's Intelligence,"[17] Manent reminds contemporary Christians that the rational creature, exercising the cardinal virtues, including the high virtue of

15  Ibid., 88–90.
16  Ibid., 88.
17  See Manent's luminous discussion of the relationship between natural law and eternal law, Providence and human prudence, in the appendix to *Natural Law and Human Rights*, "Recovering Law's Intelligence," 119–30, esp. 128–30.

prudence, is himself an essential element and instrument of divine Providence. Natural law is thus a crucial dimension of eternal law, as St. Thomas reminds us in question 91 of the "Treatise on Law." The Christian is thus obliged to overcome passivity and to exercise political responsibility in a way that avoids both radical relativism and radical secularism, on the one hand, and quietistic and theocratic contempt for the moral agency of Christians and citizens, on the other. Coming full circle, in the spirit of Corneille, Péguy, and now with a more political or prudent rendering of St. Thomas, Manent assures us that guided by Thomas's insights, Christians must "have more confidence in our practical reason and more esteem for our task."[18] We must take pride in our God-given natural gifts as responsible citizens and moral agents. Passivity, and the quietism that informs it, is an abdication of our moral and civic responsibilities, responsibilities commanded and ordained by Providence itself. This unforced meeting of Providence and prudence arises not from *a priori* theological categories, but through a lived engagement with the requirements of reflective choice itself.

## Beyond Integralism and Radical Secularism

In his luminous reflections on these themes in his 2016 book *Beyond Radical Secularism* (2015 for the French edition), Manent firmly rejects the twin extremes of integralist or theocratic politics, and a radical secularism that loses sight of the goods and motives of the human soul and that ignores or even shows contempt for what he calls the "Christian mark"[19] of European and Western nations such as France. France, for example, cannot successfully defend itself against Islamist extremism if it defines itself as a secular wasteland without a political or spiritual history that predates the revolutionary nihilist carnival of May 1968. To be sure, the secular state ought to be cherished by defenders of civic peace and civic freedom. The

---

18    Ibid., 128.

19    For Manent's discussion of the enduring "Christian mark" of Europe, which need not contradict the institutional separation of church and state, see Pierre Manent, *Beyond Radical Secularism*, trans. Ralph C. Hancock, with introduction by Daniel J. Mahoney (South Bend, IN: St. Augustine's Press, 2016), 19, 99–100, 109, 112, and 115.

original separation of church and state, religion and politics, "was once necessary" and it "remains salutary."[20] But the liberal order is fast losing confidence in the intimate connection between truth and liberty. It "has at bottom only one defect: it tends to be indifferent to truth."[21] But what a consequential deficit that is. It is losing its soul as the denizens of liberty without law, and moralistic and censorious relativism, are increasingly intolerant toward "those who are worried about the truth." Such liberty without truth is hardly worthy of human beings. About that the Socratic and the Christian can surely agree.

Reason loses its substance and efficacy when the various goods of life become innocuous "values," neither true nor false in themselves, and making no real claims on our souls. In a "Lenten Lecture" at Notre Dame Cathedral on February 25, 2007, Manent suggested that faith now "takes refuge, and sometimes shrivels," in the interior of the "heart, and tends to become confused with religious sentiment—more and more sentimental, less and less religious."[22] Many Christians thus confuse charity with tenderness and indiscriminate compassion, and the "religion of humanity" with its plans for limitless this-worldly transformation, with the Gospel of Christ.[23] As a result, deep confusion reigns in our polities, our churches, and our souls.

Some political theologians, such as John Milbank, wish to replace the liberal order with a vaguely religious state having a strikingly social democratic, even politically progressive, coloration. Anti-bourgeois ire and a one-sided communitarianism, leads to an indulgence toward a hypermodern

20  Ibid., 61–65.
21  Pierre Manent, "The Grandeur and Misery of Liberalism," trans. Paul Seaton and Daniel J. Mahoney, *Modern Age* (Summer 2011): 176–183, esp. concluding page.
22  On the increasingly tenuous relationship between truth and liberty, and religion and reason in late modernity, see Manent's "A Lenten Lecture at Notre-Dame of Paris" (delivered on Sunday, February 25, 2007), trans. Ralph C. Hancock for *Modern Age*. See also Manent, "Conversion," *Commentaire* 31 (2008): 61–62. I have drawn from both pieces.
23  See Pierre Manent's foreword to Daniel J. Mahoney, *The Idol of Our Age: How the Religion of Humanity Subverts Christianity* (New York: Encounter Books, 2018), xvii–xxi.

leftism or progressivism. One can consult any number of Milbank's books to see this logic at work. In contrast, Manent wishes to preserve the liberal political order and the secular state while rejecting the political philosophy that has led it to moral confusion, political passivity, and distrust of its own "Christian mark." Liberals have much to learn from their pre-modern European forebears who aimed "to govern [themselves] by the guidance of [their own] reason and with attention to grace." Our forebears appreciated that "it was necessary to find a place for the collaboration of human prudence and divine Providence." In that great task, "the theology of Saint Thomas Aquinas was able to provide the principles, but not to show the way to put them concretely in practice." Today, confronted by secularist sterility, moral confusion, ideological extremism, Islamist violence, and false nostalgia for clerical and confessional states, it is still necessary to renew the "covenant" between "pagan ardor and pride" in human freedom, and our "confidence in the inexhaustible and imponderable benevolence of God." With neither revolutionary nor reactionary intent, Pierre Manent reminds us that "Europe was great through" self-governing and self-limiting "nations when it was able to mix Roman virtues, courage, and prudence, with faith in a God who is friend to every person."[24] Confidence in our own powers and faith in the promises of God, greatness of soul, and humility before the Most High make a "whole" of the soul and allow a true common good to flourish "under God." It is a supreme example of high and noble *mediation* at work, a mediation rooted in reason and human experience, on the one hand, and receptivity to the self-revelation of a Provident God.

In a 2008 text published in the French traditionalist Catholic monthly *La Nef* (Manent's text was called "Liberal and Catholic"), Manent leaves us with a warning: political theology cannot lead to the reinvigoration and restoration of European and Western nations of a "Christian mark." One cannot deduce the moral foundations of free and humane political orders "from the propositions and dogmas of Christianity." One must begin with human nature and lived experience, and not the dogmatic proposition of the faith. That is precisely the false conceit of political theology in its various

---

24  All quotations in this paragraph are from Manent, *Beyond Radical Secularism*, 63–65.

forms. Whether we are speaking of "the Divine Right of Kings" or a *Marxisant* "Liberation Theology," misplaced political theologies cannot bring human freedom back into line with the requirements of the "natural order of things." "God save us from Christian utopias,"[25] Manent proclaims. Instead, statesmanship and political philosophy, informed by classical and Christian wisdom, attentiveness to the requirements of moral and political prudence, and a measured appreciation of the strengths and limits of "our temporal order," which remains to a large extent a liberal order, offer a much more promising route to the recovery and reinvigoration of a moral and political science worthy of believers and unbelievers alike. This is the most salutary path for reconnecting truth and liberty without undermining the significant achievements of the liberal order, a path outlined with clarity, sobriety, and depth in the writings of Pierre Manent. Faithful to the best resources of reason and revelation, Manent sketches a humane and viable path beyond liberal neutrality, radical secularism, pseudo-Christian humanitarianism, and forms of Christian utopianism from liberation theology on the left to integralist nostalgia for clerical authoritarianism on the right. It is a path worthy of our deepest consideration. And it is one that escapes the "terrible simplifications" of the age.

25  All quotations in this paragraph are drawn from Manent, "Libéral et Catholique," in *La Nef*, July 2008.

# Chapter 11

# PIERRE MANENT AND THE RECOVERY OF THE REPUBLICAN SPIRIT

In his thoughtful and lucid "Preface" to the French political philosopher Pierre Manent's essay-booklet *The Tragedy of the Republic* (Wiseblood Books, 2020), Patrick J. Deneen rightly emphasizes the multiple ways in which Manent has taken aim at "the modern temptation to empty the public arena of the essential activity of politics." For Manent, politics entails "putting reasons and actions in common," that is words and deeds together, in the remarkably suggestive words of Aristotle, the first and greatest political scientist in the Western tradition. It is the unending search for and articulation of the common good, and not agonistic and theatrical self-presentation and civic participation à la Hannah Arendt, or an undue and one-sided emphasis on conflict and enmity à la Carl Schmitt. Without in any way being insensitive to the genuine achievements of the liberal order, Manent notes, in Deneen's helpful formulation, that "a golden thread in modern political thinking and practice has been the effort to eliminate finally the need for politics, either through the temptations of totalitarianism, technocracy, or economism." While avoiding didacticism, Manent's thought and scholarship involves a two-fold effort to restore both the inescapable if tension-ridden dialectic of truth and liberty, and the "perpetual need to develop the virtues of prudence, wisdom, and moderation as the main tools of political engagement." About all that Deneen is right.

*The Tragedy of the Republic* originated as the first of an ongoing series of public lectures in honor of René Girard, the distinguished Franco-American social theorist, culture critic, and theorist of "mimetic desire." Delivered in French at Sciences Po in Paris, this formidable essay was translated by Ralph C. Hancock and originally appeared in *First Things*. It has recently been republished in the "Wiseblood Essays in Contemporary Culture" series from Wiseblood Books, an excellent Catholic boutique publisher specializing in the intersection of literature, religion, and social reflection faithful to broadly classical and Christian wisdom. Manent's essay, at once weighty and accessible, is worthy of sustained reflection.

For Manent, the "republic" in the original sense, is anything but passive, and demands action at the service of *la chose publique*, the commonwealth or "public thing." It is irreducibly "aristocratic" in the sense that men of talent and virtue aim to emulate each other in service to the common good. Honorable ambition is put at the service of the self-governing city. But it is also egalitarian since action informed by reason and virtue is made possible by the political realm itself, marked by "ruling and being ruled in turn," as Aristotle aptly put it. It ultimately serves, and is made possible by, a good that is truly common. To be sure, modern republicanism is *representative* in character, and thus political life takes on a much more indirect character than in the classical variant. But republicanism in any form demands action informed by moral virtue and practical reason, and not merely the articulation and defense of rights and interests, however necessary and legitimate they may be in their own sphere. Manent observes that the great modern republics, England of the 17th and 18th centuries, "a republic disguised under the form of monarchy" as Montesquieu called it in *The Spirit of the Laws*, America of the Founding era ("an extraordinary founding," Manent himself calls it), and even the France of 1789 followed by "the adventure of the Empire," were admirable expressions of political action and energy, of "emulation" among civic equals.

But modern republics, and this is coextensive with the "tragedy" that confronts them, have largely severed freedom from action informed by practical reason and civic and moral virtue. Democratic theory, as it is called in the academy, imagines liberty without command and obedience without authority; a city without citizens and states without statesmen. In this sense, the decayed modern republic knows neither civic equality nor virtuous emulation. We thus no longer know how to grasp what Manent calls "the moral bases of a truly republican regime." For a long time, the liberal commercial republic enriched and energized modern Western societies. It created a free and prosperous civil society, and a formidable state that knew how to govern. But our "reigning social philosophy"—liberalism or the ideology of human rights—mistakenly postulated that a "spontaneous social order . . . would bring together order and freedom without the mediation of political rule." Over time, this was to "abandon society to its inertia, that is, its corruption" since such a social order forgets the meaning of political rule and the citizenship and statesmanship that takes "pride in ruling for the common good." It is not a question of statism or collectivism, as some classical liberals and libertarians mistakenly think, but rather the self-government that animates, energizes, and renews a truly free society. As Manent laconically puts it, even representative republics need *to be governed* and *well governed* at that. The distinctions between authority and authoritarianism, statesmanship and tyrannical self-assertion, are at the core of free and civilized human life (about this Roger Scruton is in complete agreement). To conflate these pairs, to efface these differences, is to do great damage to the political character of human existence and the moral foundations of a free society.

To illustrate the republic in its original pre-representative form, Manent turns to Shakespeare's Roman plays, so indebted to Plutarch and through whose dramatic form the "motives of the actors of that republican regime which left the deepest mark on the history of Europe and the West" vividly come to life. Shakespeare's *Coriolanus*, Manent shows, reveals a Rome that is political through and through: "the city is the beginning and the end of all the actions of all the characters." The popular class and their tribunes are perfectly willing to honor the aristocratic greatness of the warrior hero Coriolanus; they do not object in principle to being governed by the best. But Coriolanus takes his pride, the legitimate principle of the aristocratic Roman republican regime, "to the point of insolence and furor." He refuses to show his wounds to the people, or to find the words, any words, to accompany his heroic deeds. Where the plebeians demand respect in a mixed regime, Coriolanus can only offer them "condescension and sarcasm" since "he is incapable of speaking humanely or calmly to members of the popular class." Coriolanus is the exemplar par excellence of magnanimity without moderation. He is finally not a political man since he desires to be Roman Consul without the approval of his fellow citizens. Coriolanus does not aim to be a tyrant but by going beyond politics he, like tyrants ancient and modern, undermines the vital preconditions of political liberty. He does not know how to "put reasons and actions in common" in Aristotle's inimitable words.

Manent suggestively compares him with modern statesmen who were also "great citizen(s)," namely Lincoln and de Gaulle. These two great statesmen fully appreciated that "the test of the republic lies in the almost impossible task of joining speech to deed and deed to speech, each to each aptly and justly." The eloquence, "rarity," and "brevity" of Lincoln's Gettysburg Address, that noble testament to those who gave "the last full measure of devotion" to a political order, "conceived in liberty," and "dedicated to the proposition that all men are created equal" could survive and experience a "new birth of freedom," testifies to statesmanship at the service of human freedom. De Gaulle's lucid call on June 18, 1940, for his compatriots to rally behind him to defend the liberty, honor, and independence of France, even after the Nazi conquest of the homeland, crystallizes every sentiment of noble or honorable resistance. As Manent puts it elsewhere, authentic republican heroism depends on a "more than human blending of pride and humility." In this weaving together of noble action and speech which rallies all the resources of the soul, in this unforced melding of "magnanimity and moderation," lies true human greatness. Such greatness transcends democratic categories and conventions even as it elevates democracy through the sheer fact of being itself.

Manent's treatment of Shakespeare's *Julius Caesar* is equally insightful. I will allow the reader the pleasure of making his way through both Manent's and Shakespeare's texts. But let me highlight a few particularly evocative points that Manent makes along the way. Manent shows how apolitical the Stoic Brutus's virtue really is: he cares far more about *appearing* virtuous than in doing what is necessary to root out Caesar's despotism and to revivify the Roman Republic. In particular, he resists Cassius's suggestion that the conspirators kill Marc Antony, too, since his survival surely means the survival of Caesarism. Manent also respectfully but firmly resists René Girard's suggestion that Cassius, the true "initiator" of the conspiracy against Julius Caesar, the one who "pushes against all the others," is first and foremost a "mediator of hate." Manent suggests that Girard's interpretation of the play is far too apolitical and fails to recognize "that there are noble and base hatreds." As Manent writes, "a very honorable and moral tradition, one, I must emphasize, that is Christian as well as pagan, holds that hatred for the tyrant is a noble hatred, and that it belongs to the virtue of the good citizen." As Manent argues in his autobiographical book of interviews *Seeing*

*Things Politically*, Girard is wrong to believe that "all political situations come down to the same situation." Girard sees only undifferentiated violence where there remain meaningful moral and political distinctions. Girard's anthropology of the human condition risks giving rise to passivity and civic indifference, all in the name of a misunderstanding of both Christianity and political life. "Mimetic desire" does not provide the key for understanding political life. "Mimetic desire" does not provide the key for understanding political life.

Let us return to Patrick Deneen's accurate evocation of the centrality of the cardinal virtues for Manent's vision of thought and action. For Manent, action is never an end in itself but must always be guided by the virtues. As Manent argues in *Natural Law and Human Rights*, there is such a thing as "right action, whose declensions are courage, justice, prudence, and temperance—in brief, action that takes on its form and color according to the catalogues of virtues." Here Manent channels and renews core insights of Aristotle, Cicero, and St. Thomas and perhaps Tocqueville, too. We moderns must recover an understanding of "commanding action" which is always "the commandment of right action" guided by right reason. It is the opposite of willfulness. Such action initiates and commands, but is never merely arbitrary. It is action informed by practical reason and the cardinal virtues. Deneen gets one thing wrong in his admirable "Preface" to Manent's essay: Manent does not envision a *new* republic, or a rejection of liberal *institutions*. Rather, he wants to reinvigorate those institutions by recovering a true understanding of the wellsprings of thought and action. This is a tall order, indeed, but perhaps the most promising way out of our ever-deepening modern crisis. As Wilson Carey McWilliams (a teacher and scholar esteemed by both Deneen and myself) once wrote, one of the preeminent tasks today for all those who love truth and civilization is to "bring old gods," the full weight of classical and Christian wisdom, "to a new city." That injunction perfectly describes Manent's project as I understand it. It is a liberal conservative vision *par excellence*.

# A FINAL WORD

I will leave it to the reader to flesh out further implications of the acts of recovery contained in the works of Pierre Manent and Roger Scruton. By largely complementary paths, the French political philosopher and the English philosopher and man of letters clear away the ideological obstacles, so willful and distorting, that obscure the richness (and fragility) of civilized human existence. Against the reigning spirit of repudiation, they recover a horizon of human dignity rooted in gratitude and indebtedness. Man is neither an "autonomous" being nor a helpless plaything of historical and sociological forces. This dual affirmation allows moral and civic agency to be informed by salutary self-criticism, without degenerating into pathological self-loathing. On its part, the late modern stance of repudiation can only lead to mediocrity and spiritual degradation, or absurd efforts at human self-deification. And efforts at self-deification inevitably culminate in human self-enslavement. In positive contrast, Manent and Scruton reaffirm the dignity of self-government within a territorial democracy, where free men and women combine transgenerational loyalties with the ongoing requirements of political consent. To recur to Manent's categories, Western democracy at its best aims to bring together "communion" and "consent." Or as Scruton insists, the primordial contract is between the living, the dead, and the yet to be born. Each generation never truly begins anew.

There are of course differences between Manent and Scruton, which are at once real, substantive, and subtle. In his writings, Scruton is more likely to emphasize the man-made character of law in a "society of strangers," the strictly *civil* character of civil association, in contrast to the imperatives of non-negotiable Divine Law and "submission" that mark the Islamic *ummah*. But Scruton is no radical secularist. To the contrary, he "looks back to the spiritual inheritance of Christianity, and to the two great laws of Christ, who commanded us to love God entirely and to love our neighbor as ourselves." The proper conjugation of communion and consent,

153

man-made law and deference to the sacred or holy things, demands a rejection of religious fundamentalism, Islamist fanaticism, *and* a radical secularism that ignores the needs of the soul and the requirements of civic and human "communion." To ignore, or worse reject, "the Christian mark" of Europe is to display rank impiety and ingratitude. It also leaves freedom bereft of higher ends and purposes and thus at the mercy of an excessive engrossment in everyday life, or frenzied ideological activism.

But territorial democracy of the sort extolled by Manent and Scruton is being replaced by what Manent calls "pure democracy," "a democracy without a people," where administrative rules, rights without a grounding in tradition and law, and egalitarian fantasies are "detached from any collective deliberation." Democracy becomes an abstract and increasingly illiberal project inseparable from the culture of repudiation. Only "the global," "the universal," or "the humanitarian" (as in the idea of "Humanity") have any real moral legitimacy for Western elites. Real human beings of course still live in nations, but those nations are looked down upon for being based, however tenuously, upon "borders and separations." The moral dignity of Western nations is barely acknowledged today and is even actively disparaged. Instead, Manent argues, each nation "wages war on itself," and is "no longer capable of celebrating its victories and its accomplishments." Where predecessors rightly saw the triumph of liberty under law in a self-governing community, self-hating elites see only an "inventory of crimes." As Scruton put the matter, the territorial nation—that great instrument for bringing together the secular state and the precious Christian inheritance, tradition and self-government—is "repugnant to leftists, above all intellectuals," who can find in it only "racism, ethnocentrism, and xenophobia." The Left which used to claim to represent the working classes, now despise them as "racists and xenophobes." Today members of the Left are increasingly the people "from nowhere" who despise civic loyalty as an evil. Deriding "communion" in all its forms, they have little tolerance for democratic consent either. After all, who needs the consent of racists and xenophobes? Pure democracy is thus shadowed by an ideological Manicheism reminiscent of twentieth-century totalitarianism. It is becoming more coercive, more censorious, with each passing year.

Let us end, however, on a positive note, on a note of affirmation. The fashionable theory behind the culture of repudiation, what we have called *la pensée de soixante-huit*, sees in the human world an artificial and oppressive "construct" to be forever negated and "deconstructed." In striking contrast to these false and unlivable claims, Manent and Scruton counter with two vital truths. They reaffirm that authority is not authoritarianism and, as Scruton has put it, that "power is sometimes decent and benign, like the power of a loving parent, conferred by the object of love." And both acknowledge a structure of reality that is not closed to the possibilities of the Good. Limning its various elements, they help recover a common world where humanity may find a home. And more, while doing so, they recognize those intimations of transcendence that inspire noble action and give human beings reasonable grounds for hope. Something really is better than nothing.

## Sources and Suggested Readings

In this "Final Word" I have drawn on Pierre Manent's essay, "Retrouver l'intériorité politique" and Roger Scruton's essay "Le primat de la société." Both were delivered at a colloquium of the Institut Thomas More in Paris on May 20 and 21, 2019. They subsequently appeared in *Démocratie et la liberté: Les Peuples modernes à l'épreuve de leurs contradictions*, edited by Chantal Delsol and Giulio de Ligio and published by Éditions du Cerf in 2020.

Scruton's fullest and most persuasive critique of the "heresy of domination" can be found in chapters eleven and twelve of his *An Intelligent Person's Guide to Modern Culture* (St. Augustine's Press, 2000), especially pp. 126–32.

# INDEX

Absolutism of ideology, 41–42
abstract theory, 12–13
accountability, 10–12, 14–15, 58, 60
62, 118, 132–33
*Against the Tide* (Dooley), 17, 130–35
American conservatives, 59–60
*anamnesis*, 57
"Anatomy of a Reticence" (Havel), 57
*ancien regime*, 92
Anglican Church, 14, 122
Antichrist, 119
anti-communism, 131
anti-historicism, 24
anti-modernism, 29, 36, 93
antinomianism, 8, 10, 38–44, 51, 59,
125
anti-Semitism, 16, 43, 90, 134
antitotalitarianism, 8, 38, 44, 57, 68
69, 108, 121, 134, 136, 140
Arab Islamic world, 67
Arab Spring of 2011, 61
architecture, 13
*avant-garde*, 30, 43
Arendt, Hannah, 148
Aristotle, 10, 11, 15, 91, 94, 137,
140–41, 148–52
Arnold, Matthew, 56
Aron, Raymond, 20, 22–24, 38–44,
47, 55, 86, 88–89, 93, 118–19,
136
associative habits, 62, 63
atheism, 8, 57, 119. *See also* new atheists
Augustine, 24–25
authentic individuality, 61

authenticity, 37, 77, 128
authoritarianism, 59, 147, 150, 155
authoritative institutions, 29, 35, 38,
40, 44, 50, 55, 59–62, 86
authority of the self, 124–25
autonomy, individual, 29, 61, 81,
128, 142, 143, 153
autonomy project, 82–85

Badiou, Alain, 38
barbarism, 117, 128
*Beauty* (Scruton), 13, 117
Benda, Václav, 57,103, 111
Benedict XVI (pope), 44, 67
Bénéton, Philippe, 39, 44–47, 51
Besançon, Alain, 23, 91–92
*Beyond Radical Secularism* (Manent),
33, 48, 144
bourgeois civilization, 55, 112
bourgeois ethic, 92–93
bourgeois freedom, 83
bourgeois individualism, 37, 82
bourgeois universalism, 90
Brague, Rémi, 52, 140
Brenda, Clavicle, 57, 103, 111
British Academy and the Royal Society
of Literature, 16
British architecture and town plan-
ning, 134
Brokenshire, James, 16
Building Better, Building Beautiful
Commission, 16
Burke, Edmund, 8, 10, 12, 15, 58–59,
64, 106